Junior Great Books

SERIES 2

FIRST SEMESTER

◆   ◆   ◆

AN INTERPRETIVE READING, WRITING,

AND DISCUSSION CURRICULUM

JUNIOR GREAT BOOKS

SERIES 2   FIRST SEMESTER

THE GREAT BOOKS FOUNDATION
A nonprofit educational corporation

Published and distributed by

THE GREAT BOOKS FOUNDATION
A nonprofit educational corporation

35 East Wacker Drive, Suite 2300

Chicago, IL 60601-2298

CONTENTS

Everyone was the happy lion's friend.

THE HAPPY LION

Louise Fatio

There was once a very happy lion.

His home was not the hot and dangerous plains of Africa where hunters lie in wait with their guns, it was a lovely French town with brown tile roofs and gray shutters.

The happy lion had a house in the town zoo, all for himself, with a large rock garden surrounded by a moat, in the middle of a park with flower beds and a bandstand.

···

Early every morning, François, the keeper's son, stopped on his way to school to say, "*Bonjour,* Happy Lion."

Afternoons, Monsieur Dupont, the schoolmaster, stopped on his way home to say, "*Bonjour,* Happy Lion."

Evenings, Madame Pinson, who knitted all day on the bench by the bandstand, never left without saying, "*Au revoir,* Happy Lion."

On summer Sundays, the town band filed into the bandstand to play waltzes

•••

and polkas. And the happy lion closed his
eyes to listen. He loved music. Everyone
was his friend and came to say *"Bonjour"*
and offer meat and other tidbits.

He *was* a happy lion.

One morning, the happy lion found
that his keeper had forgotten to close
the door of his house.

"Hmm," he said, "I don't like that.
Anyone may walk in."

*Why doesn't
the lion like
the idea that
anyone could
walk into
his house?*

11

"Oh well," he added on second thought, "maybe I will walk out myself and see my friends in town. It will be nice to return their visits."

So the happy lion walked out into the park and said, "*Bonjour*, my friends" to the busy sparrows.

"*Bonjour*, Happy Lion," answered the busy sparrows.

And he said, "*Bonjour*, my friend" to the quick red squirrel who sat on his tail and bit into a walnut.

"*Bonjour*, Happy Lion," said the red squirrel, hardly looking up.

• • •

Then the happy lion went into the cobblestone street where he met Monsieur Dupont just around the corner.

"Bonjour," he said, nodding in his polite lion way. "Hooooooooohhh . . ." answered Monsieur Dupont, and fainted onto the sidewalk.

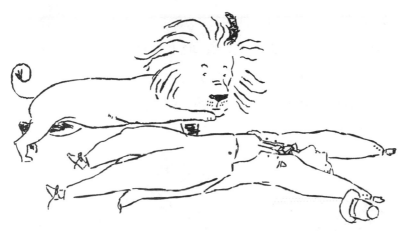

"What a silly way to say *bonjour,"* said the happy lion, and he padded along on his big soft paws.

"Bonjour, Mesdames," the happy lion said farther down the street when he saw three ladies he had known at the zoo.

"Huuuuuuuuuuuuuhhhhhh . . ." cried the three ladies, and ran away as if an ogre were after them.

"I can't think," said the happy lion, "what makes them do that. They are always so polite at the zoo."

"*Bonjour,* Madame." The happy lion nodded again when he caught up with Madame Pinson near the grocery store.

"Oo la la . . . !" cried Madame Pinson, and threw her shopping bag full of vegetables into the lion's face.

"A-a-a-a-choooooo," sneezed the lion. "People in this town are foolish, as I begin to see."

Why doesn't the lion get angry when Madame Pinson throws her shopping bag in his face?

•••

Now the lion began to hear the joyous sounds of a military march. He turned around the next corner, and there was the town band, marching down the street between two lines of people.

Ratatatum ratata ratatatum ratatata boom boom.

Before the lion could even nod and say, *"Bonjour,"* the music became screams and yells.

What a hubbub!

Musicians and spectators tumbled into one another in their flight toward doorways and sidewalk cafes. Soon the street was empty and silent.

The lion sat down and meditated. "I suppose," he said, "this must be the way people behave when they are not at the zoo."

Then he got up and went on with his stroll in search of a friend who would not faint, or scream, or run away. But the only people he saw were pointing at him excitedly from the highest windows and balconies.

Now what
was this new noise
the lion heard?

"Toootoooooot . . .
hooootooooootooooot . . ."
went the noise.

"Hooooottoooooo
TOOOOOOOOOOHHHOOOOT . . ."
and it grew more and more noisy.

"It may be the wind," said the lion.
"Unless it is the monkeys from the
zoo, all of them taking a stroll."

All of a sudden a big red fire engine
burst out of a side street and came to
a stop not too, too far from the lion.
Then a big van came backing up on the
other side of him with its back door
wide open.

The lion just sat down very quietly,
for he did not want to miss what was
going to happen.

The firemen got off the fire engine
and advanced very, very slowly toward
the lion, pulling their big fire hose along.

16

Very slowly they came closer . . . and closer . . . and the fire hose crawled on like a long snake, longer and longer. . . .

SUDDENLY, behind the lion, a little voice cried, "*Bonjour,* Happy Lion."

It was François, the keeper's son, on his way home from school! He had seen the lion and had come running to him.

The happy lion was so VERY HAPPY to meet a friend who did not run and who said *"Bonjour"* that he forgot all about the firemen.

Why does the lion's happiness make him forget all about the firemen?

17

...

And he never found out what they were going to do, because François put his hand on the lion's great mane and said, "Let's walk back to the park together."

"Yes, let's," purred the happy lion.

So François and the happy lion walked back to the zoo.

The firemen followed behind in the fire engine, and the people on the balconies and in the high windows shouted at last, "BONJOUR! HAPPY LION!"

From then on the happy lion got the best tidbits the town saved for him. But if you opened the door he would not wish to go out visiting again. He was happier to sit in his rock garden while on the other side of the moat Monsieur Dupont, Madame Pinson, and all his old friends came again like polite and sensible people to say "*Bonjour,* Happy Lion."

•••

But he was happiest when he saw
François walk through the park every
afternoon on his way home from school.
Then he swished his tail for joy, for
François remained always his dearest
friend.

· *Nutkin had no respect.* ·

THE TALE OF SQUIRREL NUTKIN

Beatrix Potter

This is a Tale about a tail—a tail that belonged to a little red squirrel, and his name was Nutkin.

He had a brother called Twinkleberry, and a great many cousins: they lived in a wood at the edge of a lake.

In the middle of the lake there is an island covered with trees and nut bushes; and amongst those trees stands a hollow oak tree, which is the house of an owl who is called Old Brown.

•••

One autumn when the nuts were
ripe, and the leaves on the hazel bushes
were golden and green—Nutkin and
Twinkleberry and all the other little
squirrels came out of the wood,
and down to the edge of the lake.

They made little rafts out of twigs,
and they paddled away over the water
to Owl Island to gather nuts.

Each squirrel had a little sack and a large oar, and spread out his tail for a sail.

They also took with them an offering of three fat mice as a present for Old Brown, and put them down upon his doorstep.

Then Twinkleberry and the other little squirrels each made a low bow, and said politely—

"Old Mr. Brown, will you favour us with permission to gather nuts upon your island?"

But Nutkin was excessively impertinent in his manners. He bobbed up and down like a little red *cherry,* singing—

"Riddle me, riddle me, rot-tot-tote!
A little wee man, in a red red coat!
A staff in his hand, and a stone in his throat;
If you'll tell me this riddle, I'll give you
      a groat."

Now this riddle is as old as the hills; Mr. Brown paid no attention whatever to Nutkin.

He shut his eyes obstinately and went to sleep.

Do you agree that Nutkin is being impertinent, or do you think he's just trying to be friendly to Old Brown?

•••

The squirrels filled their little sacks with nuts, and sailed away home in the evening.

But next morning they all came back again to Owl Island; and Twinkleberry and the others brought a fine fat mole, and laid it on the stone in front of Old Brown's doorway, and said—

"Mr. Brown, will you favour us with your gracious permission to gather some more nuts?"

But Nutkin, who had no respect, began to dance up and down, tickling old Mr. Brown with a *nettle* and singing—

"Old Mr. B! Riddle-me-ree!
  Hitty Pitty within the wall,
  Hitty Pitty without the wall;
  If you touch Hitty Pitty,
  Hitty Pitty will bite you!"

Mr. Brown woke up suddenly and carried the mole into his house.

He shut the door in Nutkin's face.
Presently a little thread of blue *smoke*
from a wood fire came up from the
top of the tree, and Nutkin peeped
through the keyhole and sang—

"A house full, a hole full!
And you cannot gather a bowl-full!"

The squirrels searched for nuts all over
the island and filled their little sacks.

But Nutkin gathered oak-apples—
yellow and scarlet—and sat upon a beech
stump playing marbles, and watching
the door of old Mr. Brown.

On the third day the squirrels got up
very early and went fishing; they caught
seven fat minnows as a present for
Old Brown.

They paddled over the lake and landed
under a crooked chestnut tree on Owl
Island.

Twinkleberry and six other little squirrels each carried a fat minnow; but Nutkin, who had no nice manners, brought no present at all. He ran in front, singing—

"The man in the wilderness said to me,
  'How many strawberries grow in the sea?'
  I answered him as I thought good—
  'As many red herrings as grow in the wood.'"

But old Mr. Brown took no interest in riddles—not even when the answer was provided for him.

On the fourth day the squirrels brought a present of six fat beetles, which were as good as plums in *plum-pudding* for Old Brown. Each beetle was wrapped up carefully in a dock-leaf, fastened with a pine-needle pin.

But Nutkin sang as rudely as ever—

"Old Mr. B! riddle-me-ree
  Flour of England, fruit of Spain,
  Met together in a shower of rain;
  Put in a bag tied round with a string,
  If you'll tell me this riddle,
      I'll give you a ring!"

Which was ridiculous of Nutkin, because he had not got any ring to give to Old Brown.

•••

The other squirrels hunted up and down the nut bushes; but Nutkin gathered robin's pincushions off a briar bush, and stuck them full of pine-needle pins.

On the fifth day the squirrels brought a present of wild honey; it was so sweet and sticky that they licked their fingers as they put it down upon the stone. They had stolen it out of a bumble *bees'* nest on the tippitty top of the hill.

But Nutkin skipped up and down, singing—

"Hum-a-bum! buzz! buzz! Hum-a-bum buzz!
  As I went over Tipple-tine
  I met a flock of bonny swine;
  Some yellow-nacked, some yellow backed!
  They were the very bonniest swine
  That e'er went over Tipple-tine."

Old Mr. Brown turned up his eyes in disgust at the impertinence of Nutkin. But he ate up the honey!

Why isn't Nutkin worried about getting in trouble with Old Brown?

❧

•••

The squirrels filled their little sacks
with nuts.

But Nutkin sat upon a big flat rock,
and played ninepins with a crab apple
and green fir-cones.

On the sixth day, which was Saturday, the squirrels came again for the last time; they brought a new-laid *egg* in a little rush basket as a last parting present for Old Brown.

But Nutkin ran in front laughing, and shouting—

"Humpty Dumpty lies in the beck,
　With a white counterpane round his neck,
　Forty doctors and forty wrights,
　Cannot put Humpty Dumpty to rights!"

Now old Mr. Brown took an interest
in eggs; he opened one eye and shut
it again. But still he did not speak.

Nutkin became more and more
impertinent—

"Old Mr. B! Old Mr. B!
Hickamore, Hackamore, on the King's
    kitchen door;
All the King's horses, and all the King's men,
Couldn't drive Hickamore, Hackamore,
Off the King's kitchen door."

Nutkin danced up and down like a
sunbeam; but still Old Brown said
nothing at all.

Nutkin began again—

"Arthur O'Bower has broken his band,
He comes roaring up the land!
The King of Scots with all his power,
Cannot turn Arthur of the Bower!"

Nutkin made a whirring noise to sound like the *wind,* and he took a running jump right onto the head of Old Brown! . . .

Then all at once there was a flutterment and a scufflement and a loud "Squeak!"

The other squirrels scuttered away into the bushes.

When they came back very cautiously, peeping round the tree—there was Old Brown sitting on his door-step, quite still, with his eyes closed, as if nothing had happened.

•   •   •   •   •

But Nutkin was in his waistcoat pocket!

This looks like the end of the story; but it isn't.

•••

Old Brown carried Nutkin into his house, and held him up by the tail, intending to skin him; but Nutkin pulled so very hard that his tail broke in two, and he dashed up the staircase and escaped out of the attic window.

And to this day, if you meet Nutkin up a tree and ask him a riddle, he will throw sticks at you, and stamp his feet and scold, and shout—

"Cuck-cuck-cuck-cur-r-r-cuck-k-k!"

Do you feel sorry for Nutkin, or do you think he gets what he deserves?

There was a Camel, most 'scruciating idle.

How the Camel Got His Hump

Rudyard Kipling

Now this tale tells how the Camel got his big hump.

In the beginning of years, when the world was so new-and-all, and the Animals were just beginning to work for Man, there was a Camel, and he lived in the middle of a Howling Desert because he did not want to work; and besides, he was a Howler himself. So he ate sticks and thorns and tamarisks and milkweed and prickles, most 'scruciating idle, and when anybody spoke to him he said, "Humph!" Just "Humph!" and no more.

Presently the Horse came to him on Monday morning, with a saddle on his back and a bit in his mouth, and said, "Camel, O Camel, come out and trot like the rest of us."

"Humph!" said the Camel, and the Horse went away and told the Man.

Presently the Dog came to him, with a stick in his mouth, and said, "Camel, O Camel, come and fetch and carry like the rest of us."

"Humph!" said the Camel, and the Dog went away and told the Man.

Presently the Ox came to him, with the yoke on his neck, and said, "Camel, O Camel, come and plough like the rest of us."

⋯

"Humph!" said the Camel, and the Ox went away and told the Man.

At the end of the day the Man called the Horse and the Dog and the Ox together and said, "Three, O Three, I'm very sorry for you (with the world so new-and-all); but that Humph-thing in the Desert can't work, or he would have been here by now, so I am going to leave him alone, and you must work double time to make up for it."

Why does the Man tell the Three that they must work double time to make up for the Camel's idleness?

•••

That made the Three very angry (with the world so new-and-all), and they held a palaver, and an *indaba,* and a *punchayet,* and a pow-wow on the edge of the Desert; and the Camel came, chewing milkweed *most* 'scruciating idle, and laughed at them. Then he said, "Humph!" and went away again.

Presently there came along the Djinn in charge of All Deserts, rolling in a cloud of dust (Djinns always travel that way because it is Magic), and he stopped to palaver and pow-wow with the Three.

"Djinn of All Deserts," said the Horse, "*is* it right for anyone to be idle, with the world so new-and-all?"

"Certainly not," said the Djinn.

"Well," said the Horse, "there's a thing in the middle of your Howling Desert (and he's a Howler himself) with a long neck and long legs, and he hasn't done a stroke of work since Monday morning. He won't trot."

•••

"Whew!" said the Djinn, whistling. "That's my Camel, for all the gold in Arabia! What does he say about it?"

"He says 'Humph!'" said the Dog, "and he won't fetch and carry."

"Does he say anything else?"

"Only 'Humph!,' and he won't plough," said the Ox.

"Very good," said the Djinn. "I'll humph him if you will kindly wait a minute."

The Djinn rolled himself up in his dust-cloak, and took a bearing across the desert, and found the Camel most 'scruciatingly idle, looking at his own reflection in a pool of water.

"My long and bubbling friend," said the Djinn, "what's this I hear of your doing no work, with the world so new-and-all?"

"Humph!" said the Camel.

The Djinn sat down, with his chin in his hand, and began to think a Great Magic, while the Camel looked at his own reflection in the pool of water.

"You've given the Three extra work ever since Monday morning, all on account of your 'scruciating idleness," said the Djinn, and he went on thinking Magics, with his chin in his hand.

"Humph!" said the Camel.

"I shouldn't say that again if I were you," said the Djinn, "you might say it once too often. Bubbles, I want you to work."

And the Camel said, "Humph!" again; but no sooner had he said it than he saw his back, that he was so proud of, puffing up and puffing up into a great big lolloping hump.

"Do you see that?" said the Djinn. "That's your very own humph that you've brought upon your very own self by not working. Today is Thursday, and you've done no work since Monday, when the work began. Now you are going to work."

"How can I," said the Camel, "with this humph on my back?"

"That's made a-purpose," said the
Djinn, "all because you missed those
three days. You will be able to work now
for three days without eating, because
you can live on your humph; and don't
you ever say I never did anything for you.
Come out of the Desert and go to the
Three, and behave. Humph yourself!"

•••

And the Camel humphed himself, humph and all, and went away to join the Three. And from that day to this the Camel always wears a humph (we call it "hump" now, not to hurt his feelings); but he has never yet caught up with the three days that he missed at the beginning of the world, and he has never yet learned how to behave.

Why doesn't the Camel ever catch up with the three days of work he missed at the beginning of the world?

How do we become like the Camel when we have too little to do? (Underline one or two things on these pages that help you answer this question.)

⚡

The Camel's hump is an ugly lump
    Which well you may see at the Zoo;
But uglier yet is the hump we get
    From having too little to do.

Kiddies and grownups too-oo-oo,
If we haven't enough to do-oo-oo,
    We get the hump—
    Cameelious hump—
The hump that is black and blue!

We climb out of bed with a frouzly head
    And a snarly-yarly voice.
We shiver and scowl and we grunt and we growl
    At our bath and our boots and our toys;

And there ought to be a corner for me
(And I know there is one for you)
    When we get the hump—
    Cameelious hump—
The hump that is black and blue!

The cure of this ill is not to sit still,
   Or frowst with a book by the fire;
But to take a large hoe and a shovel also,
   And dig till you gently perspire;

And then you will find that the sun and the wind,
And the Djinn of the Garden too,
    Have lifted the hump—
    The horrible hump—
The hump that is black and blue!

I get it as well as you-oo-oo—
If I haven't enough to do-oo-oo—
    We all get hump—
    Cameelious hump—
Kiddies and grownups too!

They all went out to look for Kanga.

Kanga and Baby Roo Come to the Forest, and Piglet Has a Bath

A. A. Milne

Nobody seemed to know where they came from, but there they were in the Forest: Kanga and Baby Roo. When Pooh asked Christopher Robin, "How did they come here?" Christopher Robin said, "In the Usual Way, if you know what I mean, Pooh," and Pooh, who didn't, said "Oh!" Then he nodded his head twice and said, "In the Usual Way. Ah!" Then he went to call upon his friend Piglet to see what *he* thought about it. And at Piglet's house he found Rabbit. So they all talked about it together.

"What I don't like about it is this," said Rabbit. "Here are we—you, Pooh, and you, Piglet, and Me—and suddenly——"

"And Eeyore," said Pooh.

"And Eeyore—and then suddenly——"

"And Owl," said Pooh.

"And Owl—and then all of a sudden——"

"Oh, and Eeyore," said Pooh. "I was forgetting *him*."

"Here—we—are," said Rabbit very slowly and carefully, "all—of—us, and then, suddenly, we wake up one morning and, what do we find? We find a Strange Animal among us. An animal of whom we have never even heard before! An animal who carries her family about with her in her pocket! Suppose *I* carried *my* family about with me in *my* pocket, how many pockets should I want?"

"Sixteen," said Piglet.

"Seventeen, isn't it?" said Rabbit. "And one more for a handkerchief—that's eighteen. Eighteen pockets in one suit! I haven't time."

There was a long and thoughtful silence . . . and then Pooh, who had been frowning very hard for some minutes, said: "*I* make it fifteen."

"What?" said Rabbit.

"Fifteen."

"Fifteen what?"

"Your family."

"What about them?"

Pooh rubbed his nose and said that he thought Rabbit had been talking about his family.

"Did I?" said Rabbit carelessly.

"Yes, you said——"

"Never mind, Pooh," said Piglet impatiently.

"The question is, What are we to do about Kanga?"

"Oh, I see," said Pooh.

"The best way," said Rabbit, "would be this. The best way would be to steal Baby Roo and hide him, and then when Kanga says, 'Where's Baby Roo?' we say, *'Aha!'*"

"*Aha!*" said Pooh, practising. "*Aha! Aha!* . . . Of course," he went on, "we could say 'Aha!' even if we hadn't stolen Baby Roo."

"Pooh," said Rabbit kindly, "you haven't any brain."

"I know," said Pooh humbly.

"We say *'Aha!'* so that Kanga knows that *we* know where Baby Roo is. *'Aha!'* means 'We'll tell you where Baby Roo is, if you promise to go away from the Forest and never come back.' Now don't talk while I think."

Pooh went into a corner and tried saying "Aha!" in that sort of voice. Sometimes it seemed to him that it did mean what Rabbit said, and sometimes it seemed to him that it didn't. "I suppose it's just practice," he thought. "I wonder if Kanga will have to practise too so as to understand it."

"There's just one thing," said Piglet, fidgeting a bit. "I was talking to Christopher Robin, and he said that a Kanga was Generally Regarded as One of the Fiercer Animals. I am not frightened of Fierce Animals in the ordinary way, but it is well known that, if One of the Fiercer Animals is Deprived of Its Young, it becomes as fierce as Two of the Fiercer Animals. In which case *'Aha!'* is perhaps a *foolish* thing to say."

"Piglet," said Rabbit, taking out a pencil, and licking the end of it, "you haven't any pluck."

"It is hard to be brave," said Piglet, sniffing slightly, "when you're only a Very Small Animal."

Rabbit, who had begun to write very busily, looked up and said, "It is because you are a very small animal that you will be Useful in the adventure before us."

Piglet was so excited at the idea of being Useful that he forgot to be frightened anymore, and when Rabbit went on to say that Kangas were only Fierce during the winter months, being at other times of an Affectionate Disposition, he could hardly sit still, he was so eager to begin being useful at once.

Why is Piglet excited by the idea of being Useful?

❧

"What about me?" said Pooh sadly.
"I suppose *I* shan't be useful?"

"Never mind, Pooh," said Piglet
comfortingly. "Another time perhaps."

"Without Pooh," said Rabbit solemnly
as he sharpened his pencil, "the adventure
would be impossible."

"Oh!" said Piglet, and tried not to look
disappointed. But Pooh went into a
corner of the room and said proudly to
himself, "Impossible without Me!
That sort of Bear."

"Now listen all of you," said Rabbit
when he had finished writing, and Pooh
and Piglet sat listening very eagerly
with their mouths open. This was what
Rabbit read out:

PLAN TO CAPTURE BABY ROO

1. *General Remarks.* Kanga runs faster than any of Us, even Me.

2. *More General Remarks.* Kanga never takes her eye off Baby Roo, except when he's safely buttoned up in her pocket.

3. *Therefore.* If we are to capture Baby Roo, we must get a Long Start, because Kanga runs faster than any of Us, even Me. (*See* 1.)

4. *A Thought.* If Roo had jumped out of Kanga's pocket and Piglet had jumped in, Kanga wouldn't know the difference, because Piglet is a Very Small Animal.

5. Like Roo.

6. But Kanga would have to be looking the other way first, so as not to see Piglet jumping in.

7. *See* 2.

8. *Another Thought.* But if Pooh was talking to her very excitedly, she *might* look the other way for a moment.

9. And then I could run away with Roo.

10. Quickly.

11. *And Kanga wouldn't discover the difference until Afterwards.*

Well, Rabbit read this out proudly, and for a little while after he had read it nobody said anything. And then Piglet, who had been opening and shutting his mouth without making any noise, managed to say very huskily:

"And—Afterwards?"

"How do you mean?"

"When Kanga *does* Discover the Difference?"

"Then we all say *'Aha!'*"

"All three of us?"

"Yes."

"Oh!"

"Why, what's the trouble, Piglet?"

"Nothing," said Piglet, "as long as *we all three* say it. As long as we all three say it," said Piglet, "I don't mind," he said, "but I shouldn't care to say *'Aha!'* by myself. It wouldn't sound *nearly* so well. By the way," he said, "you *are* quite sure about what you said about the winter months?"

"The winter months?"

"Yes, only being Fierce in the Winter Months."

"Oh, yes, yes, that's all right. Well, Pooh? You see what you have to do?"

"No," said Pooh Bear. "Not yet," he said. "What *do* I do?"

"Well, you just have to talk very hard to Kanga so as she doesn't notice anything."

"Oh! What about?"

"Anything you like."

"You mean like telling her a little bit of poetry or something?"

"That's it," said Rabbit. "Splendid. Now come along."

So they all went out to look for Kanga.

Kanga and Roo were spending a quiet afternoon in a sandy part of the Forest. Baby Roo was practising very small jumps in the sand, and falling down mouse-holes and climbing out of them, and Kanga was fidgeting about and saying, "Just one more jump, dear, and then we must go home." And at that moment who should come stumping up the hill but Pooh.

"Good afternoon, Kanga."

"Good afternoon, Pooh."

"Look at me jumping," squeaked Roo, and fell into another mouse-hole.

"Hallo, Roo, my little fellow!"

"We were just going home," said Kanga. "Good afternoon, Rabbit. Good afternoon, Piglet."

Rabbit and Piglet, who had now come up from the other side of the hill, said, "Good afternoon," and "Hallo, Roo," and Roo asked them to look at him jumping, so they stayed and looked.

And Kanga looked too. . . .

"Oh, Kanga," said Pooh, after Rabbit had winked at him twice, "I don't know if you are interested in Poetry at all?"

"Hardly at all," said Kanga.

"Oh!" said Pooh.

"Roo, dear, just one more jump and then we must go home."

There was a short silence while Roo fell down another mouse-hole.

"Go on," said Rabbit in a loud whisper behind his paw.

"Talking of Poetry," said Pooh, "I made up a little piece as I was coming along. It went like this. Er—now let me see——"

"Fancy!" said Kanga. "Now Roo, dear——"

"You'll like this piece of poetry," said Rabbit.

"You'll love it," said Piglet.

"You must listen very carefully," said Rabbit.

"So as not to miss any of it," said Piglet.

"Oh, yes," said Kanga, but she still looked at Baby Roo.

"*How* did it go, Pooh?" said Rabbit.

Pooh gave a little cough and began.

···

LINES WRITTEN BY A BEAR OF VERY LITTLE BRAIN

On Monday, when the sun is hot
I wonder to myself a lot:
"Now is it true, or is it not,
"That what is which and which is what?"

On Tuesday, when it hails and snows,
The feeling on me grows and grows
That hardly anybody knows
If those are these or these are those.

On Wednesday, when the sky is blue,
And I have nothing else to do,
I sometimes wonder if it's true
That who is what and what is who.

On Thursday, when it starts to freeze
And hoar-frost twinkles on the trees,
How very readily one sees
That these are whose—but whose are these?

On Friday——

"Yes, it is, isn't it?" said Kanga, not waiting to hear what happened on Friday. "Just one more jump, Roo, dear, and then we really *must* be going."

Rabbit gave Pooh a hurrying-up sort of nudge.

"Talking of Poetry," said Pooh quickly, "have you ever noticed that tree right over there?"

"Where?" said Kanga. "Now, Roo——"

"Right over there," said Pooh, pointing behind Kanga's back.

"No," said Kanga. "Now jump in, Roo, dear, and we'll go home."

"You ought to look at that tree right over there," said Rabbit. "Shall I lift you in, Roo?" And he picked up Roo in his paws.

"I can see a bird in it from here," said Pooh. "Or is it a fish?"

"You ought to see that bird from here," said Rabbit. "Unless it's a fish."

"It isn't a fish, it's a bird," said Piglet.

"So it is," said Rabbit.

"Is it a starling or a blackbird?" said Pooh.

"That's the whole question," said Rabbit. "Is it a blackbird or a starling?"

And then at last Kanga did turn her head to look. And the moment that her head was turned, Rabbit said in a loud voice "In you go, Roo!" and in jumped Piglet into Kanga's pocket, and off scampered Rabbit, with Roo in his paws, as fast as he could.

"Why, where's Rabbit?" said Kanga, turning round again. "Are you all right, Roo, dear?"

Piglet made a squeaky Roo-noise from the bottom of Kanga's pocket.

"Rabbit had to go away," said Pooh. "I think he thought of something he had to go and see about suddenly."

"And Piglet?"

"I think Piglet thought of something at the same time. Suddenly."

"Well, we must be getting home," said Kanga. "Goodbye, Pooh." And in three large jumps she was gone.

Pooh looked after her as she went.

...

"I wish I could jump like that," he thought. "Some can and some can't. That's how it is."

But there were moments when Piglet wished that Kanga couldn't. Often, when he had had a long walk home through the Forest, he had wished that he were a bird, but now he thought jerkily to himself at the bottom of Kanga's pocket,

        this   take
"If   is   shall   really   to
           flying I   never   it."
And as he went up in the air, he said,
"*Ooooooo!*" and as he came down he said,

"Ow!" And he was saying, *"Ooooooo-ow, Ooooooo-ow, Ooooooo-ow"* all the way to Kanga's house.

Of course as soon as Kanga unbuttoned her pocket, she saw what had happened. Just for a moment, she thought she was frightened, and then she knew she wasn't, for she felt quite sure that Christopher Robin would never let any harm happen to Roo. So she said to herself, "If they are having a joke with me, I will have a joke with them."

"Now then, Roo, dear," she said, as she took Piglet out of her pocket. "Bedtime."

"Aha!" said Piglet, as well as he could after his Terrifying Journey. But it wasn't a very good *"Aha!"* and Kanga didn't seem to understand what it meant.

"Bath first," said Kanga in a cheerful voice.

"Aha!" said Piglet again, looking round anxiously for the others. But the others weren't there. Rabbit was playing with Baby Roo in his own house,

...

and feeling more fond of him every minute, and Pooh, who had decided to be a Kanga, was still at the sandy place on the top of the Forest, practising jumps.

"I am not at all sure," said Kanga in a thoughtful voice, "that it wouldn't be a good idea to have a *cold* bath this evening. Would you like that, Roo, dear?"

Piglet, who had never been really fond of baths, shuddered a long indignant shudder, and said in as brave a voice as he could:

"Kanga, I see the time has come to speak plainly."

"Funny little Roo," said Kanga, as she got the bathwater ready.

"I am *not* Roo," said Piglet loudly. "I am Piglet!"

Why does Piglet decide that it's time to tell Kanga that he is Piglet and not Roo?

"Yes, dear, yes," said Kanga soothingly. "And imitating Piglet's voice too! So clever of him," she went on, as she took a large bar of yellow soap out of the cupboard. "What *will* he be doing next?"

"Can't you *see*?" shouted Piglet. "Haven't you got *eyes*? Look at me!"

"I *am* looking, Roo, dear," said Kanga rather severely. "And you know what I told you yesterday about making faces. If you go on making faces like Piglet's, you will grow up to *look* like Piglet—and *then* think how sorry you will be. Now then, into the

bath, and don't let me have to speak to you about it again."

Before he knew where he was, Piglet was in the bath, and Kanga was scrubbing him firmly with a large lathery flannel.

"Ow!" cried Piglet. "Let me out! I'm Piglet!"

"Don't open the mouth, dear, or the soap goes in," said Kanga. "There! What did I tell you?"

"You—you—you did it on purpose," spluttered Piglet, as soon as he could speak again . . . and then accidentally had another mouthful of lathery flannel.

"That's right, dear, don't say anything," said Kanga, and in another minute Piglet was out of the bath, and being rubbed dry with a towel.

"Now," said Kanga, "there's your medicine, and then bed."

"W-w-what medicine?" said Piglet.

"To make you grow big and strong, dear. You don't want to grow up small and weak like Piglet, do you? Well, then!"

At that moment there was a knock at the door.

"Come in," said Kanga, and in came Christopher Robin.

"Christopher Robin, Christopher Robin!" cried Piglet. "Tell Kanga who I am! She keeps saying I'm Roo. I'm *not* Roo, am I?"

Christopher Robin looked at him very carefully, and shook his head.

"You can't be Roo," he said, "because I've just seen Roo playing in Rabbit's house."

···

"Well!" said Kanga. "Fancy that! Fancy my making a mistake like that."

"There you are!" said Piglet. "I told you so. I'm Piglet."

Christopher Robin shook his head again.

"Oh, you're not Piglet," he said. "I know Piglet well, and he's *quite* a different colour."

Piglet began to say that this was because he had just had a bath, and then he thought that perhaps he wouldn't say that, and as he opened his mouth to say something else, Kanga slipped the medicine spoon in, and then patted him on the back and told him that it was really quite a nice taste when you got used to it.

"I knew it wasn't Piglet," said Kanga. "I wonder who it can be."

"Perhaps it's some relation of Pooh's," said Christopher Robin. "What about a nephew or an uncle or something?"

Kanga agreed that this was probably what it was, and said that they would have to call it by some name.

"I shall call it Pootel," said Christopher Robin. "Henry Pootel for short."

And just when it was decided, Henry Pootel wriggled out of Kanga's arms and jumped to the ground. To his great joy Christopher Robin had left the door open. Never had Henry Pootel Piglet run so fast as he ran then, and he didn't stop running until he had got quite close to his house. But when he was a hundred yards away he stopped running, and rolled the rest of the way home, so as to get his own nice comfortable colour again. . . .

Why does Piglet want to become "his own nice comfortable colour again"?

···

So Kanga and Roo stayed in the Forest.
And every Tuesday Roo spent the day
with his great friend Rabbit, and every
Tuesday Kanga spent the day with her
great friend Pooh, teaching him to jump,
and every Tuesday Piglet spent the day
with his great friend Christopher Robin.
So they were all happy again.

It was hot. The rains had not yet come.

ARAP SANG AND THE CRANES

African folktale
as told by Humphrey Harman

Arap Sang was a great chief and more than half a god, for in the days when he lived great chiefs were always a little mixed up with the gods. One day he was walking on the plain admiring the cattle.

It was hot. The rains had not yet come. The ground was almost bare of grass and as hard as stone. The thorn trees gave no shade for they were just made of long spines and thin twigs and tiny leaves and the sun went straight through them.

It was hot. Only the black ants didn't feel it and they would be happy in a furnace.

...

Arap Sang was getting old and the sun beat down on his bald head (he was sensitive about this and didn't like it mentioned) and he thought: "I'm feeling things more than I used to."

And then he came across a vulture sitting in the crotch of a tree, his wings hanging down and his eyes on the lookout.

"Vulture," said Arap Sang, "I'm hot and the sun is making my head ache. You have there a fine pair of broad wings. I'd be most grateful if you'd spread them out and let an old man enjoy a patch of shade."

"Why?" croaked Vulture. He had indigestion.

Vultures usually have indigestion; it's the things they eat.

"Why?" said Arap Sang mildly.

78

"Now that's a question to which I'm not certain that I've got the answer. Why? Why, I suppose, because I ask you. Because I'm an old man and entitled to a little assistance and respect. Because it wouldn't be much trouble to you. Because it's pleasant and good to help people."

"Bah!" said Vulture.

"What's that?"

"Oh, go home, Baldy, and stop bothering people; it's hot."

Arap Sang straightened himself up and his eyes flashed. He wasn't half a god for nothing and when he was angry he could be rather a terrible old person. And he was very angry now. It was that remark about his lack of hair.

The really terrifying thing was that when he spoke he didn't shout. He spoke quietly and the words were clear and cold and hard. And all separate like hailstones.

Why does Vulture's remark about baldness make Arap Sang especially angry?

79

•••

"Vulture," he said, "you're cruel and you're selfish. I shan't forget what you've said and you won't either. NOW GET OUT!"

Arap Sang was so impressive that Vulture got up awkwardly and flapped off.

"Silly old fool," he said uncomfortably.

Presently he met an acquaintance of his (vultures don't have friends, they just have acquaintances) and they perched together on the same bough. Vulture took a close look at his companion and then another and what he saw was so funny that it cheered him up.

"Hee, hee!" he giggled. "What's happened to you? Met with an accident? You're *bald*."

The other vulture looked sour, but at the same time you felt he might be pleased about something.

"That's good, coming from you," he said. "What have you been up to? You haven't got a feather on you above the shoulders."

Then they both felt their heads
with consternation. It was quite true.
They were bald, both of them, and so
was every other vulture, the whole
family, right down to this very day.

Which goes to show that if you can't
be ordinarily pleasant to people at
least it's not wise to go insulting great
chiefs who are half gods.

I said that he was rather a terrible
old person.

Arap Sang walked on. He was feeling shaky. Losing his temper always upset him afterward, and doing the sort of magic that makes every vulture in the world bald in the wink of an eye takes it out of you if you aren't as young as you used to be.

And he *did* want a bit of shade.

Presently he met an elephant. Elephant was panting across the plain in a tearing hurry and was most reluctant to stop when Arap Sang called to him.

···

"Elephant," said Arap Sang weakly. "I'm tired and I'm dizzy. I want to get to the forest and into a bit of shade but it's a long way."

"It *is* hot, isn't it?" said Elephant. "I'm off to the forest myself."

"Would you spread out your great ears and let me walk along under them?" asked Arap Sang.

"I'm sorry," said Elephant, "but you'd make my journey so slow. I must get to the forest. I've got the most terrible headache."

"Well, I've got a headache too," protested the old man.

"I'm sure," said Elephant, "and no one could be sorrier about that than I am. Is it a very big headache?"

"Shocking big," said Arap Sang.

"There now," said Elephant. "Consider how big I am compared to you and what the size of *my* headache must be."

What's wrong with Elephant's excuse for not helping Arap Sang?

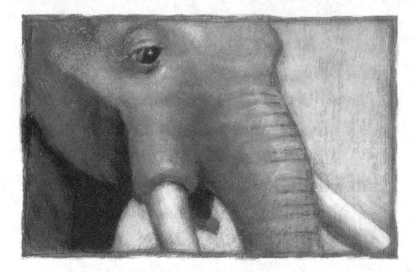

That's elephants all over, always so logical. Arap Sang felt that there was something wrong with this argument but he couldn't just see where. Also he had become a little uncomfortable about all those bald vultures and he didn't want to lose his temper with anyone else. You have to be careful what you do when you're half a god. It's so dreadfully final.

"Oh, all right," he muttered.

"Knew you'd see it that way," said Elephant. "It's just what I was saying about you the other day. You can always rely on Arap Sang, I said, to behave reasonably. Well, goodbye and good luck."

···

And he hurried off in the direction
of the distant forest and was soon
out of sight.

Poor Arap Sang was now feeling very
ill indeed. He sat on the ground and he
thought to himself: "I can't go another
step unless I get some shade and if I
don't get some soon I'm done for."

And there he was found by a flock
of cranes.

They came dancing through the white
grass, stamping their long delicate legs so
that the insects flew up in alarm and
were at once snapped up in the cranes'
beaks. They gathered round Arap Sang
sitting on the ground and he looked
so old and distressed that they
hopped up and down
with embarrassment,

first on one leg, then the other. "Korong! Korong!" they called softly and this happens to be their name as well.

"Good birds," whispered Arap Sang, "you must help me. If I don't reach shade soon I'll die. Help me to the forest."

"But, of course," said the cranes, and they spread their great handsome black and white wings to shade him and helped him to his feet, and together, slowly, they all crossed the plain into the trees.

Then Arap Sang sat in the shade of a fine cotton tree and felt very much better. The birds gathered round him and he looked at them and thought that he had never seen more beautiful creatures in the whole world.

"And kind. Kind as well as beautiful," he muttered. "The two don't always go together. I must reward them."

"I shan't forget your kindness," he said, "and I'll see that no one else does. Now I want each one of you to come here."

Then the cranes came one after another and bowed before him and Arap Sang stretched out his kindly old hand and gently touched each beautiful sleek head. And where he did this a golden crown appeared and after the birds had gravely bowed their thanks they all flew off to the lake, their new crowns glittering in the evening sun.

Arap Sang felt quite recovered. He was very pleased with his gift to the cranes.

Why is Arap Sang "very pleased" with his gift to the cranes?

...

Two months later a crane dragged himself to the door of Arap Sang's house. It was a pitiful sight, thin with hunger, feathers broken and muddy from hiding in the reeds, eyes red with lack of sleep.

Arap Sang exclaimed in pity and horror.

"Great Chief," said the crane, "we beg you to take back your gift. If you don't there'll soon be not one crane left alive for we are hunted day and night for the sake of our golden crowns."

Arap Sang listened and nodded his head in sorrow.

"I'm old and I'm foolish," he said, "and I harm my friends. I had forgotten that men also were greedy

and selfish and that they'll do anything
for gold. Let me undo the wrong I
have done by giving without thought.
I'll make one more magic but that'll
be the last."

Then he took their golden crowns and
in their place he put a wonderful halo of
feathers which they have until this day.

But they still are called Crowned
Cranes.

The moose ate seventeen bowls of chowder.

Blue Moose

Daniel Manus Pinkwater

MOOSE MEETING

Mr. Breton had a little restaurant
on the edge of the big woods. There
was nothing north of Mr. Breton's house
except nothing, with trees in between.
When winter came, the north wind blew
through the trees and froze everything
solid. Then it would snow. Mr. Breton
didn't like it.

Mr. Breton was a very good cook.
Every day, people from the town came
to his restaurant. They ate gallons of

···

his special clam chowder. They ate plates of his special beef stew. They ate fish stew and Mr. Breton's special homemade bread. The people from the town never talked much and they never said anything about his cooking.

"Did you like your clam chowder?" Mr. Breton would ask.

"Yup," the people from the town would say.

Mr. Breton wished they would say, "Delicious!" or, "Good chowder, Breton!" All they ever said was, "Yup." In winter they came on skis and snowshoes.

Every morning Mr. Breton went out behind his house to get firewood. He wore three sweaters, a scarf, galoshes, a woolen hat, a big checkered coat, and mittens. He still felt cold. Sometimes animals came out of the woods to watch Mr. Breton. Raccoons and rabbits came. The cold didn't bother them. It bothered Mr. Breton even more when they watched him.

•••

One morning there was a moose in Mr.
Breton's yard. It was a blue moose. When
Mr. Breton went out his back door, the
moose was there, looking at him. After a
while, Mr. Breton went back in, closed
the door, and made a pot of coffee while
he waited for the moose to go away.
It didn't go away; it just stood in Mr.
Breton's yard, looking at his back door.

Mr. Breton drank a cup of coffee. The moose stood in the yard. Mr. Breton opened the door again. "Shoo! Go away!" he said.

"Do you mind if I come in and get warm?" the moose said. "I'm just about frozen." The moose brushed past him and walked into the kitchen. His antlers almost touched the ceiling.

The moose sat down on the floor next to Mr. Breton's stove. He closed his eyes and sat leaning toward the stove for a long time. Mr. Breton stood in the kitchen, looking at the moose. The moose didn't move. Wisps of steam began to rise from his blue fur. After a long time the moose sighed. It sounded like a foghorn.

"Can I get you a cup of coffee?" Mr. Breton asked the moose. "Or some clam chowder?"

"Clam chowder," said the moose.

Mr. Breton filled a bowl with creamy clam chowder and set it on the floor.

The moose dipped his big nose into the bowl and snuffled up the chowder. He made a sort of slurping, whistling noise.

"Sir," the moose said, "this is wonderful clam chowder."

Mr. Breton blushed a very deep red. "Do you really mean that?"

"Sir," the moose said, "I have eaten some very good chowder in my time, and yours is the very best."

"Oh my," said Mr. Breton, blushing even redder. "Oh my. Would you like some more?"

"Yes, with crackers," said the moose.

The moose ate seventeen bowls of chowder with crackers. Then he had twelve pieces of hot gingerbread and forty-eight cups of coffee. While the moose slurped and whistled, Mr. Breton sat in a chair. Every now and then he said to himself, "Oh my. The best he's ever eaten. Oh my."

Later, when some people from the town came to Mr. Breton's house, the moose met them at the door. "How many in your party, please?" the moose asked. "I have a table for you; please follow me."

The people from the town were surprised to see the moose. They felt like running away, but they were too surprised. The moose led them to a table, brought them menus, looked at each person, snorted, and clumped into the kitchen.

"There are some people outside; I'll take care of them," he told Mr. Breton.

The people were whispering to one another about the moose, when he clumped back to the table.

"Are you ready to order?"

"Yup," the people from the town said. They waited for the moose to ask them if they would like some chowder, the way Mr. Breton always did. But the moose just stared at them as though they were very foolish. The people felt uncomfortable. "We'll have the clam chowder."

"Chaudière de Clam; very good," the moose said. "Do you desire crackers or homemade bread?"

"We will have crackers," said the people from the town.

"I suggest you have the bread; it is hot," said the moose.

"We will have bread," said the people from the town.

"And for dessert," said the moose, "will you have fresh gingerbread or Apple Jacquette?"

"What do you recommend?" asked the people from the town.

"After the Chaudière de Clam, the gingerbread is best."

"Thank you," said the people from the town.

"It is my pleasure to serve you," said the moose. The moose brought bowls of chowder balanced on his antlers.

At the end of the meal, the moose clumped to the table. "Has everything been to your satisfaction?" he asked.

•••

"Yup," said the people from the town, their mouths full of gingerbread.

"I beg your pardon?" said the moose. "What did you say?"

"It was very good," said the people from the town. "It was the best we've ever eaten."

"I will tell the chef," said the moose.

The moose clumped into the kitchen and told Mr. Breton that the people from the town had said that the food was the best they had ever eaten. Mr. Breton rushed out of the kitchen and out of the house. The people from the town were sitting on the porch, putting on their snowshoes.

"Did you tell the moose that my clam chowder was the best you've ever eaten?" Mr. Breton asked.

"Yup," said the people from the town, "we said that. We think that you are the best cook in the world; we have always thought so."

"Always?" asked Mr. Breton.

"Of course," the people from the town said. "Why do you think we walk seven miles on snowshoes just to eat here?"

The people from the town walked away on their snowshoes. Mr. Breton sat on the edge of the porch and thought it over. When the moose came out to see why Mr. Breton was sitting outside without his coat on, Mr. Breton said, "Do you know, those people think I am the best cook in the whole world?"

"Of course they do," the moose said. "Do you want me to go into town to get some crackers? We seem to have run out."

"Yes," said Mr. Breton, "and get some asparagus too. I'm going to cook something special tomorrow."

"By the way," said the moose, "aren't you cold out here?"

"No, I'm not the least bit cold," Mr. Breton said. "This is turning out to be a very mild winter."

Why doesn't Mr. Breton feel cold once the townspeople tell him he's the best cook in the world?

101

GAME WARDEN

There was a lot of talk in town about the moose at Mr. Breton's restaurant. Some people who had never been there before went to the restaurant just to see the moose. There was an article in the newspaper about the moose, and how

he talked to the customers, and brought them their bowls of clam chowder, and helped Mr. Breton in the kitchen.

Some people from other towns drove a long way with chains on their tires to Mr. Breton's restaurant, just to see the moose. Mr. Breton was always very busy waiting on tables at lunchtime and suppertime.

The moose was always very polite to the people, but he made them feel a little uncomfortable too. He looked at people with only one eye at a time, and he was better than most of them at pronouncing French words. He knew what kind of wine to drink with clam chowder, and he knew which kind of wine to drink with the special beef stew. Some of the people in the town bragged that the moose was a friend of theirs, and always gave them a table right away. When they came to the restaurant they would pat the moose on the back, and say, "Hello, Moose, you remember me, don't you?"

···

"There will be a slight delay until a table is ready," the moose would say, and snort, and shake himself.

Mr. Breton was very happy in the kitchen. There were pots of all sorts of good things steaming on the stove and smelling good, and bread baking in the oven from morning to night. Mr. Breton loved to cook good things for lots of people, the more the better. He had never been so busy and happy in his life.

One morning, Mr. Bobowicz, the game warden, came to the restaurant. "Mr. Breton, are you aware of Section 5— Subheading 6—Paragraph 3 of the state fish and game laws?" said Mr. Bobowicz.

"No, I am not aware of Section 5— Subheading 6—Paragraph 3," Mr. Breton said. "What is it all about?"

"No person shall keep a moose as a pet, tie up a moose, keep a moose in a pen or barn, or parlor or bedroom, or any such enclosure," said Mr. Bobowicz.

"In short, it is against the law to have
a tame moose."

"Oh my," said Mr. Breton, "I don't
want to do anything against the law. But
I don't keep the moose. He just came
along one day, and has stayed ever since.
He helps me run my restaurant."

Mr. Bobowicz rubbed his chin. "And
where is the aforesaid moose?"

Mr. Breton had given the moose one
of the rooms upstairs, in which there was
a particularly large bed. The moose just
fit in the bed, if he folded up his feet.

He liked it very much; he said he never
had a bed of his own. The moose slept on
the bed under six blankets, and during

the day he would go upstairs sometimes, and stretch out on the bed and sigh with pleasure.

When Mr. Bobowicz came to see Mr. Breton, the moose had been downstairs to help Mr. Breton eat a giant breakfast, and then he had wandered back to his room to enjoy lying on his bed until the lunchtime customers arrived. He heard Mr. Breton and Mr. Bobowicz talking. The moose bugled. He had never bugled in Mr. Breton's house before. Bugling is a noise that no animal except a moose can really do right. Elk can bugle, and elephants can bugle, and some kinds of geese and swans can bugle, but it is nothing like moose bugling. When the moose bugled, the whole house jumped and rattled, dishes clinked together in the cupboard, pots and pans clanged together, icicles fell off the house.

"I AM NOT A TAME MOOSE!" the moose shouted from where he was lying on his bed.

Mr. Bobowicz looked at Mr. Breton with very wide eyes. "Was that the moose?"

The moose had gotten out of bed, and was clumping down the stairs. "You're flipping right, that was the moose," he growled.

•••

The moose clumped right up to Mr. Bobowicz, and looked at him with one red eye. The moose's nose was touching Mr. Bobowicz's nose. They just stood there, looking at each other, for a long time. The moose was breathing loudly, and his eye seemed to be a glowing coal. Mr. Bobowicz's knees were shaking. Then the moose spoke very slowly. "You . . . are . . . a . . . tame . . . game warden."

The moose turned, and clumped back up the stairs. Mr. Breton and Mr. Bobowicz heard him sigh and heard the springs crash and groan as he flopped onto the big bed.

"Mr. Bobowicz, the moose is not tame," Mr. Breton said. "He is a wild moose, and he lives here of his own free will; he is the headwaiter." Mr. Breton spoke very quietly, because Mr. Bobowicz had not moved since the moose had come downstairs. His eyes were still open very wide, and his knees were still shaking.

•••

Mr. Breton took Mr. Bobowicz by the hand, and led him into the kitchen and poured him a cup of coffee.

Why doesn't the moose want anyone to think he is "tame"?

DAVE

Not very far from Mr. Breton's house,
in a secret place in the woods, lived
a hermit named Dave. Everybody knew
that Dave was out there, but nobody
ever saw him. Mr. Bobowicz, the game
warden, had seen what might have been
Dave a couple of times; or it might have
been a shadow. Sometimes, late at
night, Mr. Breton would hear the wind
whistling strangely, and think of Dave.

The moose brought Dave home with
him one night. They were old friends.
Dave was dressed in rabbit skins, stitched
together. His feet were wrapped in tree
bark and moose-moss. An owl sat on
his head.

"Dave is very shy," the moose said.
"He would appreciate it if you didn't
say anything to him until he knows you
better, maybe in ten or fifteen years.
He knows about your gingerbread,
and he would like to try it." While the

moose spoke, Dave blushed very red,
and tried to cover his face with the owl,
which fluttered and squawked.

Mr. Breton put dishes with gingerbread
and applesauce and fresh whipped cream
in front of Dave, the moose, and the
owl. There was no noise but the moose
slurping, and Dave's spoon scraping.
Mr. Breton turned to get the coffeepot.
When he looked back at the table,
Dave and the owl were gone.

•••

"Dave says thank you," the moose said.

The next night Dave was back, and this time he had a whistle made out of a turkey bone in his hat. After the gingerbread, Dave played on the whistle,

like the wind making strange sounds, the moose hummed, and Mr. Breton clicked two spoons, while the owl hopped up and down on the kitchen table, far into the night.

Why does Dave the hermit feel comfortable in Mr. Breton's kitchen?

One day after the moose had been
staying with Mr. Breton for a fairly long
time, there was an especially heavy
snowfall. The snow got to be as high as
the house, and there was no way for
people to come from the town.

Mr. Breton got a big fire going in
the stove, and kept adding pieces of
wood until the stove was glowing red.

The house was warm, and filled with the smell of applesauce, which Mr. Breton was cooking in big pots on the stove. Mr. Breton was peeling apples and the moose was sitting on the floor, lapping every now and then at a big chowder bowl full of coffee on the kitchen table.

The moose didn't say anything. Mr. Breton didn't say anything. Now and then the moose would take a deep breath with his nose in the air, sniffing in the smell of apples and cinnamon and raisins cooking. Then he would sigh. The sighs got louder and longer.

The moose began to hum—softly, then louder. The humming made the table shake, and Mr. Breton felt the humming in his fingers each time he picked up an apple. The humming mixed with the apple and cinnamon smell and melted the frost on the windows, and the room filled with sunlight. Mr. Breton smelled flowers.

Then he could see them. The kitchen floor had turned into a meadow with new grass, dandelions, periwinkles, and daisies.

The moose hummed. Mr. Breton smelled melting snow. He heard ice cracking. He felt the ground shake under the hoofs of moose returning from the low, wet places. Rabbits bounded through the fields. Bears, thin after the winter's sleep, came out of hiding. Birds sang.

The people in the town could not remember such an unseasonable thaw. The weather got warm all of a sudden, and the ice and snow melted for four days before winter set in again. When they went to Mr. Breton's restaurant, they discovered that he had made a wonderful stew with lots of carrots that reminded them of meadows in springtime.

MOOSE MOVING

When spring finally came, the moose became moody. He spent a lot of time staring out the back door. Flocks of geese flew overhead, returning to lakes in the North, and the moose always stirred when he heard their honking.

"Chef," the moose said one morning, "I will be going tomorrow. I wonder if you would pack some gingerbread for me to take along."

Mr. Breton baked a special batch of gingerbread, and packed it in parcels tied with string, so the moose could hang them from his antlers. When the moose came downstairs, Mr. Breton was sitting in the kitchen drinking coffee. The parcels of gingerbread were on the kitchen table.

...

"Do you want a bowl of coffee before you go?" Mr. Breton asked.

"Thank you," said the moose.

"I shall certainly miss you," Mr. Breton said.

"Thank you," said the moose.

"You are the best friend I have," said Mr. Breton.

"Thank you," said the moose.

"Do you suppose you'll ever come back?" Mr. Breton asked.

"Not before Thursday or Friday," said the moose. "It would be impolite to visit my uncle for less than a week."

The moose hooked his antlers into the loops of string on the packages of gingerbread. "My uncle will like this." He stood up and turned to the door.

"Wait!" Mr. Breton shouted. "Do you mean that you are not leaving forever? I thought you were lonely for the life of a wild moose. I thought you wanted to go back to the wild, free places."

• • •

"Chef, do you have any idea of how cold it gets in the wild, free places?" the moose said. "And the food! Terrible!"

"Have a nice time at your uncle's," said Mr. Breton.

"I'll send you a postcard," said the moose.

Why did Mr. Breton think the moose was lonely for the life of a wild moose?

Anancy can't believe it's Bro Puss.

ANANCY AND DOG AND PUSS AND FRIENDSHIP

West Indian folktale
as told by James Berry

Bro Puss insists on doing the shopping, even when he's not at all fit and well.

Anancy sees Bro Puss walking down the road with a stick. Anancy can't believe it's Bro Puss with leg all bandaged up, hobbling towards him, carrying a shopping basket.

Anancy stops.

"Oh, Bro Puss, I'd say good morning. But all so hurt and bandaged up, how can it be a good morning for you?"

"You take notice, Bro Nancy," Bro Puss says. "You take notice. All the same, good morning, Bro Nancy."

"Good morning, Bro Puss. But— what bad luck has overtaken you with so much pain?"

"Ah, Bro Nancy! It's nobody else besides Bro Dog."

"Bro Dog? Bro Dog has damaged you?" Anancy is shocked.

Sad-sad, Bro Puss looks down. He nods his head and says, "Yes, Bro Nancy. Bro Dog has damaged me. Bro Dog has actually broken my leg."

"Just out of sudden badness?"

"Well," Puss says, "as you know, me and Mrs. Puss share our home duties. And few days ago, I went to the shop. I waited. I then happened to point out

...

I was first to be served. Bro Dog jumped on me. Held me. Tossed me against the wall. Next thing I knew I couldn't get up. Couldn't raise myself, Bro Nancy. Then I saw I couldn't walk at all."

"Oh, maddest madness!" Bro Nancy says. "Crazy madness! That's not like the Bro Dog I know." Bro Nancy shakes his head. "Not, not at all."

"But it is, you know," Puss says. "It is. Bro Dog's like that. I know. I know from experience."

"Bro Puss," Anancy says, "I'm sad. I'm sorry. Sorry to hear. Sad to see you like this. But—it's here in me, it's not like Bro Dog to be so vile. I have to believe a bad-bad tiger spirit rose up in Bro Dog and made him vile. Made him damaging."

"No, Bro Nancy. No," Puss says. "It's just him. It's just Bro Dog. It's just him . . . All the same—can you speak to him?"

"Speak to him?" Anancy says. "I'll go right now. I'll let Bro Dog answer to this damage he's done to you."

Why is Anancy so eager to go and speak to Bro Dog?

As Anancy speaks, his son Tacooma comes along. Tacooma says good morning to his father and Bro Puss and agrees that Dog has behaved very, very badly.

Tacooma takes the shopping basket from Bro Puss and walks to the shop with him. Anancy goes off straight to see Bro Dog.

Listen to the Anancy now, sitting down all friendly-friendly. "Bro Dog, I met a man today. You may call him Bro Kitten. And you know what has happened to Bro Kitten?"

"No," Dog says. "What?"

"Bro Lion has broken Bro Kitten's leg."

"Badness," Dog says. "Terrible badness! Lions are all the same. Wild and ignorant. What else can you expect? They get no schooling whatsoever. None."

"Bro Dog," Anancy says, "suppose I should say, the Bro Kitten is Bro Puss. And the Bro Lion is you. What would you say?"

Bro Dog goes quiet. Then Bro Dog says, "I'd say, I'm ashamed. Badly, badly ashamed."

"Ashamed enough to make the broken leg come good?"

"I can't mend broken legs. I can't, can I?"

"No, Bro Dog," Anancy says. "But you can mend a lot-lot by becoming friends."

"Me getting friendly with Puss? After breaking his leg? Would you even talk to me?"

"Bro Puss himself asked me to come and talk to you," Anancy says.

"Really?" Dog says, guilty and surprised, looking round at Anancy.

"Yes," Anancy says. "He asks me to come and talk to you."

Again Dog goes quiet, then says, "It's not the first time I hurt Bro Puss. You know that."

"Yes, Bro Dog."

"Yet," Dog says, "it seems Puss knows I feel bad I damaged him."

"Suppose," Anancy says, "both of you should meet, eye to eye, not too cross, cool-cool, with only a little bad-mind?"

"Would be all right," Dog says. "Would be good. If you can fix it up."

Anancy works as a go-between.
Anancy gets the badness between Dog
and Puss really cooled off. It even seems
all their trouble has gone—disappeared.

Every day now Bro Dog goes to the
house of Bro and Mrs. Puss. He gets
wood for them. He gets water.
He fetches and he carries practically
everything. By the time the leg of
Puss is healed up again,
he and Dog are
perfect-perfect
friends.

•••

Bro Dog and Bro Puss are seen together everywhere, doing jobs, or just enjoying themselves like old friends.

One day, Bro Dog invites Bro Puss to come to the seaside with him. Bro Puss hesitates, not really wanting to go, but still not wanting to be the first to refuse a friendly request.

They go to the seaside.

Dog promptly slips into the sea and begins to swim and dive and do all kinds of things in the water, enjoying himself. Puss sits under a coconut tree and watches Dog.

Bro Dog waves to Puss, calls him, "Come on in! Come on. The water's great!"

"I'll stay here and watch you,"
Puss calls back.

Every now and then Dog calls
to Puss inviting him to come in the
water. People on the beach
become amused by Bro Puss
and Bro Dog.

• • •

Every time Dog calls to Puss to come and try doing this or that, Puss calls back saying, "I'll stay here and watch you."

And Puss sits there and watches Dog float, dive, leap out and splash back in the water, and swim in all different kinds of ways.

As Dog comes out of the water, Puss compliments him on being such an excellent swimmer.

"Anybody can do it," Dog says. "Anybody—who isn't frightened."

"It's a talent you have," Puss says, "and I don't. That's why I sit and watch you."

"Oh, come off it," Dog says. "Anybody can swim. Anybody who isn't frightened."

Bro Puss changes the subject. Bro Puss says nothing more about his lack of talent and feeling for enjoyment in water.

Why does Bro Puss change the subject?

132

A few days later, at a holiday time, Puss specially invites Dog to a packed lunch at a well-used picnic and beauty spot.

Not having eaten, on purpose, Dog arrives hungry. All ravenous and ready to tuck into the special feast-lunch both Mrs. and Bro Puss prepared together. Yet, Bro Puss hangs about, in no hurry to open up the lunch and begin the eating.

Sitting there under a tree, Bro Dog has to wait, listening to long drawn-out tales Bro Puss tells about his family.

Then, sudden-sudden, Bro Puss picks
up the well-stuffed bag of food. He
tosses the handle round his shoulders.
He fastens himself against the tree. And,
calm-calm, Bro Puss climbs himself up
and up into the tree. Soon, Bro Puss is
sitting at ease, comfortable, in the

branches of the tree, with the bag of food.

At first, Dog doesn't understand what is happening. He's puzzled at what funny game Puss is playing. Bro Dog stands, looking up into the tree.

Bro Puss looks down and calls, "I have lunch for you, Bro Dog. Come and get it."

"What d'you mean?" Dog says. "You know very well I can't get up there. And you must know my belly's rumbling."

"Anybody can climb up," Puss says. "Anybody who isn't frightened."

Dog is shocked. Dog remembers using those words at the seaside. Dog looks down, thinking, "Oh! Puss is playing a game of teaching-a-lesson. Puss wants to trick me into seeing something!"

Dog is cross. Dog feels he has been tricked. He feels he has been invited to a special lunch so that he can be taught a lesson. Dog thinks back at the swim in the sea.

•••

Dog remembers he hasn't made a call to Puss for a swim to put him down or to give him any lesson. He has made his call to Puss to come and swim—come and enjoy the swim with him—as he has felt it.

"Things are natural when they happen as they happen," Dog tells himself. "When something happens between friends as you feel it, that's natural. But when a game is set up to catch you out, or teach you a lesson, that's a trick."

Getting hungrier and hungrier, Dog walks round the tree, looking up, and says, "Bring the food down, Bro Puss. You invite me to lunch. Come down with it."

"Come up and get it, Bro Dog," Puss says. "Climb up and get it. Anybody can do it. Anybody—who isn't frightened."

Dog sees that Puss is sitting comfortably in the tree eating his lunch.

Dog leans against the tree. Dog sits down. Dog feels like waiting just to attack Puss when he comes down, and not bother with any of the food. But Dog is so empty, it hurts.

Dog knows he cannot leave the food. Dog knows too, he cannot find it in himself to attack Puss and eat his food.

Suddenly, Puss comes down from the tree. Puss hands Dog his lunch.

⋯

Standing there, Dog takes the lunch, looking really cross with Puss. A wave of madness comes over him to attack Puss. But, instead, an enticing smell of the cooked meat under his nose makes Dog want to eat more than attack Puss.

Dog sits down. He looks up crossly at Puss, sitting there. Bro Dog picks up the enticing meat; he gobbles it, crushing up the bones. And Bro Dog goes on eating his way through his lunch, not saying a single word.

"Have you got the point, Bro Dog?" Puss says. "Do you see now . . . that different people can do different things? And . . . we have much more . . . because different people can do different things? We have bird-singing . . .

···

and frog-croaking. We have cow-mooing, and jackass-braying. We have horse-galloping, and kangaroo-jumping . . . Say you see the point. Come on, Bro Dog. Say you see the point. Some people can get about in water . . . Others can get up and around in a tree . . . Say you see my point. Say you see it!"

Dog finishes his lunch, gets up, and says, "Bro Puss, if ever we are going to manage being friends, we better keep it on the ground. And not in the sea or up in any tree. All right?"

Bro Dog walks away quickly by himself, going off in a huff.

From that time, cats and dogs keep trying to be friends.

Why does Dog say that he and Puss can be friends only if they "keep it on the ground"?

By morning they grew right up to the sky.

Jack and the Beanstalk

*English folktale
as told by Joseph Jacobs*

There was once upon a time a poor widow who had an only son named Jack and a cow named Milky-white. And all they had to live on was the milk the cow gave every morning, which they carried to the market and sold. But one morning Milky-white gave no milk and they didn't know what to do.

"What shall we do, what shall we do?" said the widow, wringing her hands.

"Cheer up, mother, I'll go and get work somewhere," said Jack.

"We've tried that before, and nobody would take you," said his mother. "We must sell Milky-white and with the money start a shop or something."

"All right, mother," says Jack. "It's market day today, and I'll soon sell Milky-white, and then we'll see what we can do."

So he took the cow's halter in his hand, and off he started. He hadn't gone far when he met a funny-looking old man who said to him: "Good morning, Jack."

"Good morning to you," said Jack, and wondered how he knew his name.

"Well, Jack, and where are you off to?" said the man.

"I'm going to market to sell our cow here."

"Oh, you look the proper sort of chap to sell cows," said the man. "I wonder if you know how many beans make five."

"Two in each hand and one in your mouth," says Jack, as sharp as a needle.

"Right you are," says the man. "And here they are, the very beans themselves," he went on, pulling out of his pocket a number of strange-looking beans. "As you are so sharp," says he, "I don't mind doing a swap with you—your cow for these beans."

"Go along," says Jack. "Wouldn't you like it?"

"Ah! you don't know what these beans are," said the man. "If you plant them overnight, by morning they grow right up to the sky."

"Really?" says Jack. "You don't say so."

"Yes, that is so, and if it doesn't turn out to be true you can have your cow back."

"Right," says Jack, and hands him over Milky-white's halter and pockets the beans.

*Would **you** trade Milky-white for the strange-looking beans? Why do you think Jack does?*

143

Back goes Jack home, and as he hadn't gone very far it wasn't dusk by the time he got to his door.

"Back already, Jack?" said his mother. "I see you haven't got Milky-white, so you've sold her. How much did you get for her?"

"You'll never guess, mother," says Jack.

"No, you don't say so. Good boy! Five pounds, ten, fifteen, no, it can't be twenty."

"I told you you couldn't guess. What do you say to these beans; they're magical, plant them overnight and—"

"What!" says Jack's mother. "Have you been such a fool, such a dolt, such an idiot, as to give away my Milky-white, the best milker in the parish, and prime beef to boot, for a set of paltry beans? Take that! Take that! Take that! And as for your precious beans, here they go out of the window. And now off with you to bed. Not a sip shall you drink, and not a bit shall you swallow this very night."

So Jack went upstairs to his little room in the attic, and sad and sorry he was, to be sure, as much for his mother's sake as for the loss of his supper.

At last he dropped off to sleep.

When he woke up, the room looked so funny. The sun was shining into part of it, and yet all the rest was quite dark and shady. So Jack jumped up and dressed himself and went to the window. And what do you think he saw? Why, the beans his mother had thrown out of the window into the garden had sprung up into a big beanstalk which went up

and up and up till it reached the sky.
So the man spoke truth after all.

The beanstalk grew up quite close past
Jack's window, so all he
had to do was to open it
and give a jump onto the
beanstalk, which ran up just
like a big ladder. So Jack
climbed, and he climbed and
he climbed and he climbed
and he climbed and he
climbed and he climbed till
at last he reached the sky.
And when he got there he
found a long broad road
going as straight as a dart.
So he walked along and he
walked along and he
walked along till he
came to a great
big tall house,
and on the
doorstep there
was a great big
tall woman.

*Would you
climb a
beanstalk that
reached to the
sky? Why do
you think
Jack does?*

...

"Good morning, mum," says Jack, quite polite-like. "Could you be so kind as to give me some breakfast?" For he hadn't had anything to eat, you know, the night before and was as hungry as a hunter.

"It's breakfast you want, is it?" says the great big tall woman. "It's breakfast you'll be if you don't move off from here. My man is an ogre and there's nothing he likes better than boys broiled on toast. You'd better be moving on or he'll soon be coming."

"Oh! please mum, do give me something to eat, mum. I've had nothing to eat since yesterday morning, really and truly, mum," says Jack. "I may as well be broiled as die of hunger."

Well, the ogre's wife was not half so bad after all. So she took Jack into the kitchen and gave him a chunk of bread and cheese and a jug of milk. But Jack hadn't half finished these when thump! thump! thump! the whole house began to tremble with the noise of someone coming.

"Goodness gracious me! It's my old man," said the ogre's wife. "What on earth shall I do? Come along quick and jump in here." And she bundled Jack into the oven just as the ogre came in.

He was a big one, to be sure. At his belt he had three calves strung up by the heels, and he unhooked them and threw them down on the table and said: "Here, wife, broil me a couple of these for breakfast. Ah! what's this I smell?

Fee-fi-fo-fum,

I smell the blood of an Englishman,

Be he alive, or be he dead

I'll grind his bones to make my bread."

"Nonsense, dear," said his wife, "you're dreaming. Or perhaps you smell the scraps of that little boy you liked so much for yesterday's dinner. Here, you go and have a wash and tidy up, and by the time you come back your breakfast will be ready for you."

So off the ogre went, and Jack was just going to jump out of the oven and run away when the woman told him not. "Wait till he's asleep," says she. "He always has a doze after breakfast."

Well, the ogre had his breakfast, and after that he goes to a big chest and takes out a couple of bags of gold, and down he sits and counts till at last his head began to nod and he began to snore till the whole house shook again.

Then Jack crept out on tiptoe from his oven, and as he was passing the ogre he took one of the bags of gold under his arm, and off he pelters till he came to the beanstalk, and then he threw down the bag of gold, which of course fell into his mother's garden, and then he climbed down and climbed down till at last he got home and told his mother and showed her the gold and said: "Well, mother, wasn't I right about the beans? They are really magical, you see."

•••

So they lived on the bag of gold for some time, but at last they came to the end of it, and Jack made up his mind to try his luck once more up at the top of the beanstalk. So one fine morning he rose up early and got onto the beanstalk, and he climbed and he climbed and he climbed and he climbed and he climbed and he climbed and he climbed till at last he came out onto the road again and up to the great big tall house he had been to before. There, sure enough, was the great big tall woman standing on the doorstep.

"Good morning, mum," says Jack, as bold as brass. "Could you be so good as to give me something to eat?"

"Go away, my boy," said the big tall woman, "or else my man will eat you up for breakfast. But aren't you the youngster who came here once before? Do you know, that very day, my man missed one of his bags of gold."

"That's strange, mum," says Jack. "I daresay I could tell you something about that, but I'm so hungry I can't speak till I've had something to eat."

Well the big tall woman was so curious that she took him in and gave him something to eat. But he had scarcely begun munching it as slowly as he could when thump! thump! thump! they heard the giant's footstep, and his wife hid Jack away in the oven.

All happened as it did before. In came the ogre as he did before, said "Fee-fi-fo-fum," and had his breakfast of three broiled oxen. Then he said: "Wife, bring me the hen that lays the golden eggs." So she brought it, and the ogre said "Lay," and it laid an egg all of gold. And then the ogre began to nod his head and to snore till the house shook.

Then Jack crept out of the oven on tiptoe and caught hold of the golden hen, and was off before you could say "Jack Robinson." But this time the hen gave a cackle which woke the ogre, and just as Jack got out of the house he heard

him calling:
"Wife, wife, what have
you done with my golden hen?"

And the wife said: "Why, my dear?"

But that was all Jack heard, for he
rushed off to the beanstalk and climbed
down like a house on fire. And when
he got home he showed his mother
the wonderful hen and said "Lay," to it;
and it laid a golden egg every time
he said "Lay."

Well, Jack was not content, and it wasn't very long before he determined to have another try at his luck up there at the top of the beanstalk. So one fine morning he rose up early, and got onto the beanstalk, and he climbed and he climbed and he climbed and he climbed till he got to the top. But this time he knew better than to go straight to

...

the ogre's house. And when he got near
it he waited behind a bush till he saw
the ogre's wife come out with a pail
to get some water, and then he crept into
the house and got into the copper. He
hadn't been there long when he heard
thump! thump! thump! as before, and
in come the ogre and his wife.

"Fee-fi-fo-fum, I smell the blood of an
Englishman," cried out the ogre. "I smell
him, wife, I smell him."

"Do you, my dearie?" says the ogre's
wife. "Then if it's that little rogue that
stole your gold and the hen that laid the
golden eggs, he's sure to have got into
the oven." And they both rushed to the
oven. But Jack wasn't there, luckily, and
the ogre's wife said: "There you are again
with your fee-fi-fo-fum. Why of course
it's the boy you caught last night that
I've just broiled for your breakfast. How
forgetful I am, and how careless you
are not to know the difference between
live and dead after all these years."

···

So the ogre sat down to the breakfast and ate it, but every now and then he would mutter: "Well, I could have sworn—" and he'd get up and search the larder and the cupboards, and everything, only luckily he didn't think of the copper.

After breakfast was over, the ogre called out: "Wife, wife, bring me my golden harp." So she brought it and put it on the table before him. Then he said "Sing!" and the golden harp sang most beautifully. And it went on singing till the ogre fell asleep and commenced to snore like thunder.

Then Jack lifted up the copper lid very quietly and got down like a mouse and crept on hands and knees till he came to the table, when up he crawled, caught hold of the golden harp, and dashed with it towards the door. But the harp called out quite loud "Master! Master!" and the ogre woke up just in time to see Jack running off with his harp.

Would you keep the harp even after it woke up the ogre? Why do you think Jack does?

Jack ran as fast
as he could, and
the ogre came rushing
after, and would soon have
caught him only Jack had a
start and dodged him a bit and knew
where he was going. When he got to the
beanstalk the ogre was not more than
twenty yards away, when suddenly he
saw Jack disappear, and when he came
to the end of the road he saw Jack
underneath climbing down for dear life.

Well, the ogre didn't like trusting himself to such a ladder, and he stood and waited, so Jack got another start. But just then the harp cried out "Master! Master!" and the ogre swung himself down onto the beanstalk, which shook with his weight.

Down climbs Jack, and after him climbed the ogre. By this time Jack had climbed down and climbed down and climbed down till he was very nearly home. So he called out: "Mother! Mother! Bring me an axe, bring me an axe." And his mother came rushing out with the axe in her hand, but when she came to the beanstalk she stood stock still with fright for there she saw the ogre with his legs just through the clouds.

But Jack jumped down and got hold
of the axe and gave a chop at the
beanstalk which cut it half in two. The
ogre felt the beanstalk shake and quiver
so he stopped to see what was the
matter. Then Jack gave another chop
with the axe, and the beanstalk
was cut in two and began to topple
over. Then the ogre fell down
and broke his crown, and
the beanstalk came
toppling after.

Then Jack showed
his mother his
golden harp, and
what with showing
that and selling the
golden eggs, Jack
and his mother
became very rich,
and he married a
great princess, and
they lived happy
ever after.

There once lived an honest old man.

THE MAGIC
LISTENING CAP

*Japanese folktale
as told by Yoshiko Uchida*

There once lived an honest old man
who was kind and good, but who was so
poor, he hardly had enough to eat each
day. What made him sadder than not
having enough to eat himself was that he
could no longer bring an offering to his
guardian god at the nearby shrine.

"If only I could bring even an offering
of fish," he thought sadly.

Finally, one day, when his house
was empty and he had nothing left to
eat, he walked to the shrine of his god.

...

He got on his knees and bowed down before him.

"I've come today to offer the only thing I have left," he said sadly. "I have only myself to offer now. Take my life if you will have it."

The old man knelt silently and waited for the god to speak.

Soon there was a faint
rumbling, and the man
heard a voice that seemed
to come from far, far away.
"Don't worry, old man,"
the god said to him. "You have
been honest and you have
been good. From today on I shall
change your fortune, and you shall
suffer no longer."

Then the guardian god gave the old
man a little red cap. "Take this cap, old
man," he said. "It is a magic listening cap.

With this on your head, you will be able to hear such sounds as you have never heard before."

The old man looked up in surprise. He was old, but he heard quite well, and he had heard many, many sounds during the long years of his life.

"What do you mean?" he asked. "What new sounds are there in this world that I have not yet heard?"

The god smiled. "Have you ever really heard what the nightingale says as it flies to the plum tree in the spring? Have you ever understood what the trees whisper to one another when their leaves rustle in the wind?"

The old man shook his head. He understood.

"Thank you, dear god," he said. "I shall treasure my magic cap forever." And carrying it carefully, he hurried toward his home.

As the old man walked along, the sun grew hot, and he stopped to rest in the

shade of a big
tree that stood at
the roadside.
Suddenly, he saw
two black crows
fly into the tree. One
came from the mountains,
and the other from the sea.
He could hear their noisy
chatter fill the air above him.
Now was the time to try his
magic cap! Quickly, he put it
on, and as soon as he did, he
could understand everything
the crows were saying.

What new things does the old man learn about nature when he puts on the magic listening cap? (Underline two or three things on these pages that help you answer this question.)

"And how is life in the land beyond the sea?" asked the mountain crow.

"Ah, life is not easy," answered the crow of the sea. "It grows harder and harder to find food for my young ones. But tell me, do you have any interesting news from the mountains?"

"All is not well in our land either," answered the crow from the mountains. "We are worried about our friend, the camphor tree, who grows weaker and weaker, but can neither live nor die."

"Why, how can that be?" asked the crow of the sea.

"It is an interesting tale," answered the mountain crow. "About six years ago, a wealthy man in our town built a guest house in his garden. He cut down the camphor tree in order to build the house, but the roots were never dug out. The tree is not dead, but neither can it live, for each time it sends new shoots out from beneath the house, they are cut off by the gardener."

"Ah, the poor tree," said the crow of the sea sympathetically. "What will it do?"

"It cries and moans constantly, but alas, human beings are very stupid," said the mountain crow. "No one seems to hear it, and it has cast an evil spell on the wealthy man and made him very ill. If they don't dig up the tree and plant it where it can grow, the spell will not be broken and the man will soon die. He has been ill a long time."

•••

The two crows sat in the tree and talked of many things, but the old man who listened below could not forget the story of the dying man and the camphor tree.

"If only I could save them both," he thought. "I am probably the only human being who knows what is making the man ill."

He got up quickly, and all the way home, he tried to think of some way in which he might save the dying man. "I could go to his home and tell him exactly what I heard," he thought. "But surely no one will believe me if I say I heard two crows talking in a tree. I must think of a clever way to be heard and believed."

As he walked along, a good idea suddenly came to him. "I shall go disguised as a fortune teller," he thought. "Then surely they will believe me."

The very next day the old man took his little red cap, and set out for the town where the sick man lived. He walked by the front gate of this man's home, calling in a loud voice, "Fortunes! Fortunes! I tell fortunes!" Soon the gate flew open and the sick man's wife came rushing out.

"Come in, old man. Come in," she called. "Tell me how I can make my husband well. I have had doctors from near and far, but not one can tell me what to do."

The old man went inside and listened to the woman's story. "We have tried herbs and medicines from many, many lands, but nothing seems to help him," she said sadly.

Then the old man said, "Did you not build a guest house in your garden six years ago?" The wife nodded. "And hasn't your husband been ill ever since?"

"Why, yes," answered the wife, nodding. "That's right. How did you know?"

•••

"A fortune teller knows many things," the old man answered, and then he said, "Let me sleep in your guest house tonight, and by tomorrow I shall be able to tell you how your husband can be cured."

"Yes, of course," the wife answered. "We shall do anything you say."

And so, that night after a sumptuous feast, the old man was taken to the guest house. A beautiful new quilt was laid out for him on the *tatami,* and a charcoal brazier was brought in to keep him warm.

*What new
things does the
old man learn
about nature
when he puts
on the magic
listening cap
this time?
(Underline two
or three things
on these pages
that help you
answer this
question.)*
❧

•••

As soon as he was quite alone, the old man put on his little red cap and sat quietly, waiting to hear the camphor tree speak. He slid open the paper doors and looked out at the sky sprinkled with glowing stars. He waited and he waited, but the night was silent and he didn't even hear the whisper of a sound. As he sat in the darkness, the old man began to wonder if the crows had been wrong.

"Perhaps there is no dying camphor tree after all," he thought. And still wearing his red cap, the old man climbed into the quilts and closed his eyes.

Suddenly, he heard a soft rustling sound, like many leaves fluttering in the wind. Then he heard a low gentle voice.

"How do you feel tonight, camphor tree?" the voice called into the silence.

Then the old man heard a hollow sound that seemed to come from beneath the floor.

"Ah, is that you, pine tree?" it asked weakly. "I do not feel well at all. I think

172

I am about to die . . . about to die . . ." it wailed softly.

Soon, another voice whispered, "It's I, the cedar from across the path. Do you feel better tonight, camphor tree?"

And one after the other, the trees of the garden whispered gently to the camphor tree, asking how it felt. Each time, the camphor tree answered weakly, "I am dying . . . I am dying. . . ."

The old man knew that if the tree died, the master of the house would also die. Early the next morning, he hurried to the bedside of the dying man. He told him about the tree and about the evil spell it had cast upon him.

"If you want to live," he said,
"have the camphor tree dug up quickly,
and plant it somewhere in your garden
where it can grow."

The sick man nodded weakly. "I will
do anything, if only I can become well
and strong again."

And so, that very morning, carpenters
and gardeners were called to come from
the village. The carpenters tore out the
floor of the guest house and found the
stump of the camphor tree. Carefully,
carefully, the gardeners lifted it out of the
earth and then moved it into the garden

where it had room to grow. The old
man, wearing his red cap, watched as the
tree was planted where the moss was
green and moist.

"Ah, at last," he heard the camphor tree
sigh. "I can reach up again to the good
clean air. I can grow once more!"

As soon as the tree was transplanted,
the wealthy man began to grow stronger.
Before long, he felt so much better he
could get up for a few hours each day.
Then he was up all day long, and, finally,
he was completely well.

"I must thank the old fortune teller for saving my life," he said, "for if he had not come to tell me about the camphor tree, I would probably not be alive today."

And so he sent for the old man with the little red cap.

"You were far wiser than any of the doctors who came from near and far to see me," he said to the old man. Then, giving him many bags filled with gold, he said, "Take this gift, and with it my life-long thanks. And when this gold is gone, I shall see that you get more."

"Ah, you are indeed very kind," the old man said happily, and taking his gold, he set off for home.

As soon as he got home, he took some of the gold coins and went to the village market. There he bought rice cakes and sweet tangerines and the very best fish he could find. He hurried with them to his guardian god, and placed them before his shrine.

"My fortunes have indeed changed since you gave me this wonderful magic cap," the old man said. "I thank you more than I can say."

Each day after that, the old man went to the shrine, and never forgot to bring an offering of rice or wine or fish to his god. He was able to live in comfort, and never had to worry again about not having enough to eat. And, because he was not a greedy man, he put away his magic listening cap and didn't try to tell any more fortunes. Instead, he lived quietly and happily the rest of his days.

If you had the magic listening cap, what would you do with it? Why?

A Jackal and a Partridge swore eternal friendship.

THE JACKAL AND THE PARTRIDGE

Punjabi folktale
as told by Flora Annie Steel

A Jackal and a Partridge swore eternal friendship; but the Jackal was very exacting and jealous. "You don't do half as much for me as I do for you," he used to say, "and yet you talk a great deal of your friendship. Now my idea of a friend is one who is able to make me laugh or cry, give me a good meal, or save my life if need be. You couldn't do that!"

"Let us see," answered the Partridge. "Follow me at a little distance, and if I don't make you laugh soon you may eat me!"

Why does the Jackal demand so much from a friend?

179

So she
flew on till she
met two travelers trudging
along, one behind the other. They
were both footsore and weary, and the
first carried his bundle on a stick over
his shoulder, while the second had
his shoes in his hand.

Lightly as a feather the Partridge settled
on the first traveler's stick. He, none the
wiser, trudged on, but the second traveler,
seeing the bird sitting so tamely just in
front of his nose, said to himself, "What
a chance for a supper!" and immediately
flung his shoes at it, they being ready
to hand. Whereupon the Partridge flew
away, and the shoes knocked off the
first traveler's turban.

"What a plague do you mean?" cried
he, angrily turning on his companion.

"Why did you
throw your shoes at my head?"

"Brother!" replied the other mildly,
"do not be vexed. I didn't throw them at
you, but at a Partridge that was sitting
on your stick."

"On my stick! Do you take me for a
fool?" shouted the injured man, in a great
rage. "Don't tell me such cock-and-bull
stories. First you insult me, and then you
lie like a coward; but I'll teach you
manners!"

Then he fell upon his fellow traveler without more ado, and they fought until they could not see out of their eyes, till their noses were bleeding, their clothes in rags, and the Jackal had nearly died of laughing.

"Are you satisfied?" asked the Partridge of her friend.

"Well," answered the Jackal, "you have certainly made me laugh, but I doubt if you could make me cry. It is easy enough to be a buffoon; it is more difficult to excite the higher emotions."

"Let us see," retorted the Partridge, somewhat piqued. "There is a huntsman with his dogs coming along the road.

Just creep into that hollow tree and watch me: if you don't weep scalding tears, you must have no feeling in you!"

The Jackal did as he was bid, and watched the Partridge, who began fluttering about the bushes till the dogs caught sight of her, when she flew to the hollow tree where the Jackal was hidden. Of course the dogs smelt him at once, and set up such a yelping and scratching that the huntsman came up, and seeing what it was, dragged the Jackal out by the tail. Whereupon the dogs worried him to their hearts' content, and finally left him for dead.

Why does the Partridge play a trick that almost kills her friend the Jackal?

By and by
he opened
his eyes—for he was only
foxing—and saw the Partridge
sitting on a branch above him.

"Did you cry?" she asked anxiously.
"Did I rouse your higher emo——"

"Be quiet, will you!" snarled the
Jackal; "I'm half dead with fear!"

So there the Jackal lay for some
time, getting the better of his bruises,
and meanwhile he became hungry.

"Now is the time for friendship!"
said he to the Partridge. "Get me a good

dinner, and I will acknowledge you are
a true friend."

"Very well!" replied the Partridge;
"only watch me, and help yourself when
the time comes."

Just then a troop of women came by,
carrying their husbands' dinners to the
harvest field.

The Partridge gave a little plaintive cry,
and began fluttering along from bush
to bush as if she were wounded.

"A wounded bird!—a wounded bird!"
cried the women.
"We can easily
catch it!"

Whereupon they
set off in pursuit,
but the cunning
Partridge played
a thousand tricks,
till they became

so excited over the chase that they put their bundles on the ground in order to pursue it more nimbly. The Jackal, meanwhile, seizing his opportunity, crept up, and made off with a good dinner.

"Are you satisfied now?" asked the Partridge.

"Well," returned the Jackal, "I confess you have given me a very good dinner; you have also made me laugh—and cry—ahem! But, after all, the great test of friendship is beyond you—you couldn't save my life!"

"Perhaps not," acquiesced the Partridge mournfully, "I am so small and weak. But it grows late—we should be going home; and as it is a long way round by the ford, let us go across the river. My friend the crocodile will carry us over."

Accordingly, they set off for the river, and the crocodile kindly consented to carry them across, so they sat on his broad back and he ferried them over. But just as they were in the middle of the stream the Partridge remarked, "I believe the crocodile intends to play us a trick. How awkward if he were to drop you into the water!"

"Awkward for you too!" replied the Jackal, turning pale.

...

"Not at all! Not at all! I have wings, you haven't."

At this the Jackal shivered and shook with fear, and when the crocodile, in a gruesome growl, remarked that he was hungry and wanted a good meal, the wretched creature hadn't a word to say.

"Pooh!" cried the Partridge airily, "don't try tricks on *us*—I should fly away, and as for my friend the Jackal, you couldn't hurt *him*. He is not such a fool as to take his life with him on these little excursions; he leaves it at home, locked up in the cupboard."

"Is that a fact?" asked the crocodile, surprised.

"Certainly!" retorted the Partridge. "Try to eat him if you like, but you will only tire yourself to no purpose."

"Dear me! How very odd!" gasped the crocodile; and he was so taken aback that he carried the Jackal safe to shore.

Do you think the Partridge is being a good friend or a bad friend here? Why?

•••

"Well, are you satisfied now?" asked
the Partridge.

"My dear madam!" quoth the Jackal,
"you have made me laugh, you have
made me cry, you have given me a good
dinner, and you have saved my life;
but upon my honor I think you are too
clever for a friend; so goodbye!"

And the Jackal never went
near the Partridge again.

All of a sudden, he saw a light up ahead.

Nail Soup

*Swedish folktale
as told by Linda Rahm*

Once, just around dusk, a poor traveler named Carl was making his way up a lonely mountain road. As the sky grew darker and the wind grew colder, Carl wondered how he was going to find shelter for the night. Then, all of a sudden, he saw a light up ahead. Walking on a little further, he discovered that the light came from a fire, and the fire was burning brightly inside a small cottage.

"How pleasant it would be to warm myself before that fire, and maybe get a little something to eat," he thought.

Just then an old woman came toward him.

"Good evening, Madam," said Carl, with a big smile.

"Good evening," said the woman, but she did not smile. "And where might you have come from?"

"Name any place you like," replied the wanderer, "for I have been all over the world, and now I'm on my way back home."

"You are a great traveler indeed," said the old woman. "But what business do you have here?"

"Now that you ask," replied Carl, "I thought you might offer me a bit of food and shelter for the night."

"Humph, I expected as much," said the old woman, "but you can just think again. My house is not an inn."

"My good lady," said Carl, "surely your heart cannot be so hard, and on a bitter night like this. Come, we are both human beings and ought to help one another."

"Help one another?" snapped the woman. "Help? And who will help me, I'd like to know. I haven't got a scrap of food in the house! No, you'll just have to find another place to stay."

Why doesn't the old woman want to help Carl?

193

But Carl was not the kind of person to give up at the first disappointment. Although the old woman continued to grumble and complain, Carl was persistent. He begged and pleaded like a starved dog, until at last she gave in and agreed to let him sleep on the floor for the night.

Carl thanked her heartily and started off toward the cottage, singing as he went:

"Better on the floor without sleep,
Than freeze upon the mountain steep."

For, you see, Carl was a jolly fellow, always ready with a rhyme.

When he came inside, Carl could see that the woman was not so badly off as she pretended. There was a roaring fire in the hearth and shiny cooking pots hanging all around it.

Carl now made himself very agreeable, and asked in his most charming manner

if she might spare him a tiny little
something to eat.

"And where am I to get it from?" cried
the old woman. "I haven't had a bite
myself this whole day!"

But Carl was a quick-witted fellow, he
was. "Poor old Granny," he said, shaking

his head sadly, "you must be starving.
Well, well, I suppose I'll just have to ask
you to have something with *me*."

"Have something with you!" exclaimed
the old woman. "You don't look as if
you could ask anyone to have anything!
What have you got to offer a body,
I should like to know?"

"North, south, west, east,
Know-how is as good as a feast.
North, south, east, west,
And he who travels most knows best,"

sang Carl gaily. "Lend me a pot, Granny!"
By this time, the old woman was
curious, as you may guess, so she
handed him a pot.
Carl filled the pot with water, put it
on the fire, and blew with all his might
until the fire blazed up even higher.
Then he brought out a small nail that
he happened to have in his pocket. Very
carefully, he placed it on the palm of his
hand and turned it around three times.

Then, Carl dropped the nail
into the pot of boiling water.

The woman stared.
"What's this going to be?"
she demanded.

"Nail soup," said Carl,
and he began to stir the
water round and round
with a wooden spoon.

"Nail soup?" asked
the woman.

"That's right. Nail soup,"
replied Carl.

The old woman had seen and
heard a good deal in her time, but
making soup with a nail! Well, she had
never heard the like before.

"That would be a useful thing for poor
people to know," she said. "I should like
to learn how to make it."

"If it's worth the having,
It's worth the trouble learning,"

said Carl. "Just watch me closely."

The old woman squatted on the ground, her hands clasping her knees and her eyes following every move of Carl's hand as he went on stirring the water.

"This generally makes delicious soup," he explained, "but tonight it may be rather thin, because I've been using the same nail all week long. Now, if we had a handful of oatmeal to put in, that would thicken it up nicely. But, of course, you don't have any food to spare, so,

> What can't be cured,
> Must be endured."

And he went on stirring the water.

Finally, the old woman muttered, "Well, I think I may have a pinch of oatmeal somewhere," and left the room. When she returned, she was carrying a whole bowlful of fine oatmeal.

Why does the old woman come back with a whole bowlful of fine oatmeal, instead of just a handful?

198

· Carl continued to stir and began
sprinkling the oatmeal into the soup,
while the woman stared wide-eyed, first
at him and then at the pot.

"Mmmmm," said Carl, sniffing the pot,
"this soup smells tasty enough for
company. Why, if we just had a bit of
beef and a few potatoes to add, it would
even be fit for gentlefolks, however fussy
they might be about their soup. But,

What can't be cured,
Must be endured."

...

Well, when the old woman set her mind to it, she thought maybe she *did* have some potatoes, and perhaps even a bit of dried beef, too. These she gave to Carl, who went on stirring and stirring, while she stared as hard as ever.

"This soup would satisfy the grandest lords and ladies in the land," declared Carl.

"Well, I never!" thought the woman. "And just imagine—all from a nail!" He really was a remarkable person, this poor wanderer!

"You know, if we had a few carrots, we could ask the king himself to dine," said Carl, "for this soup is exactly what he has every evening. I know that for a fact, because I once worked for the king's cook."

"Dear me! Invite the king to have some! Well, I never!" exclaimed the woman, slapping her knees. She was quite impressed by Carl's royal connections.

"But of course," shrugged Carl,
"you don't have any carrots, so,

What can't be cured,
Must be endured."

"Wait a minute; I just remembered
that I might have one carrot left in my
garden," said the old woman. She hurried
off and soon returned with her apron
full of carrots, plus a few turnips for
good measure.

•••

Carl went on stirring, and the old woman went on staring, one moment at him and the next moment at the pot. Then all at once Carl took out the nail with a flourish.

"It's ready," he announced. "Now we'll have a real feast. Of course, the king and the queen usually have bread and butter with this kind of soup. And, naturally, they always have a cloth on the table when they eat," he added. "But,

What can't be cured,
Must be endured."

Now by this time the old woman was beginning to feel quite grand herself. If that was all that was needed, she thought, why not, just once in her life, live like a queen? Straight to the cupboard she went, and brought out not only bread and butter, but pancakes and ale and such an array of cheeses and sausages that at last the table looked as if it had been set for a banquet.

Never in
her life had the old
woman had such a fine meal;
never had she tasted such wonderful
soup. And just think, made with only a
nail! The very idea made her laugh
with pleasure, and she couldn't praise
Carl enough for teaching her such a
useful thing.

So they ate and drank and talked, and
talked and drank and ate some more,
and then Carl asked the old woman
to dance, and they whirled around the
room until they were both worn out.

...

Carl was now going to lie down on the floor for the night. But that would never do, thought the old woman. No, that was impossible. "Such a grand person must have a bed to sleep in," she said.

Carl did not need much persuading. "It's just like the sweet Christmas time," he said, "and a nicer woman I never met. Ah, happy are travelers who meet with such generous people!" And he lay down on the spare bed and went to sleep.

•••

The next morning when he woke, the first thing he got was a pot of coffee and a freshly baked loaf of bread. And when he was leaving, the old woman gave him a bright silver coin.

"Many, many thanks for what you have taught me," she said. "I shall live in comfort for the rest of my days, now that I have learned how to make soup from a nail!"

"Well, it isn't very difficult, if you only have something good to add to it," said Carl as he went on his way.

"Such people don't grow on every bush," thought the old woman as she watched him disappear from sight.

Why doesn't Carl tell the old woman that the soup wasn't really made from a nail?

"Everyone who sees the apple will long for it."

THE APPLE OF CONTENTMENT

Howard Pyle

There was a woman once, and she had three daughters. The first daughter squinted with both eyes, yet the woman loved her as she loved salt, for she herself squinted with both eyes. The second daughter had one shoulder higher than the other, and eyebrows as black as soot in the chimney, yet the woman loved her as well as she loved the other, for she herself had black eyebrows and one shoulder higher than the other. The youngest daughter was as pretty as a ripe apple, and had hair as fine as silk and the color of pure gold, but the woman loved her not at all, for, as I have said, she herself was neither pretty, nor had she hair of the color of pure gold. Why all this was so, even Hans Pfifendrummel cannot tell, though he has read many books and one over.

The first sister and the second sister dressed in their Sunday clothes every day, and sat in the sun doing nothing, just as though they had been born ladies, both of them.

As for Christine—that was the name of the youngest girl—as for Christine, she dressed in nothing but rags, and had to drive the geese to the hills in the morning and home again in the evening, so that they might feed on the young grass all day and grow fat.

The first sister and the second sister had white bread (and butter beside) and as much fresh milk as they could drink, but Christine had to eat cheese-parings

and bread-crusts, and had hardly enough
of them to keep Goodman Hunger
from whispering in her ear.

This was how the churn clacked in
that house!

Well, one morning Christine started
off to the hills with her flock of geese,
and in her hands she carried her knitting,
at which she worked to save time.
So she went along the dusty road until,
by-and-by, she came to a place where
a bridge crossed the brook, and what
should she see there but a little red cap,

with a silver bell at the point of it, hanging from the alder branch. It was such a nice, pretty little red cap that Christine thought that she would take it home with her, for she had never seen the like of it in all of her life before.

So she put it in her pocket, and then off she went with her geese again. But she had hardly gone two-score of paces when she heard a voice calling her, "Christine! Christine!"

She looked, and who should she see but a queer little gray man, with a great head as big as a cabbage and little legs as thin as young radishes.

"What do you want?" said Christine, when the little man had come to where she was.

Oh, the little man only wanted his cap again, for without it he could not go back home into the hill—that was where he belonged.

But how did the cap come to be hanging from the bush? Yes, Christine would like to know that before she gave it back again.

Well, the little hill-man was fishing by the brook over yonder when a puff of wind blew his cap into the water, and he just hung it up to dry. That was all that there was about it, and now would Christine please give it to him?

Christine did not know how about that. Perhaps she would and perhaps she would not. It was a nice, pretty little cap— what would the little underground man give her for it? That was the question.

Oh, the little man would give her five thalers for it, and gladly.

No, five thalers was not enough for such a pretty little cap—see, there was a silver bell hanging to it too.

Well, the little man did not want to be hard at a bargain. He would give her a hundred thalers for it.

No, Christine did not care for money. What else would he give for this nice, dear little cap?

Why doesn't Christine care for money, when she is so poor?

211

...

"See, Christine," said the little man, "I will give you this for the cap." And he showed her something in his hand that looked just like a bean, only it was as black as a lump of coal.

"Yes, good, but what is that?" said Christine.

"That," said the little man, "is a seed from the apple of contentment. Plant it, and from it will grow a tree, and from the tree an apple. Everybody in the world that sees the apple will long for it, but nobody in the world can pluck it but you. It will always be meat and drink to you when you are hungry, and warm clothes to your back when you are cold. Moreover, as soon as you pluck it from the tree, another as good will grow in its place. *Now,* will you give me my hat?"

•••

Oh yes, Christine would give the little man his cap for such a seed as that, and gladly enough. So the little man gave Christine the seed, and Christine gave the little man his cap again. He put the cap on his head, and—puff!—away he was gone, as suddenly as the light of a candle when you blow it out.

So Christine took the seed home with her, and planted it before the window of her room. The next morning when she looked out of the window she beheld a beautiful tree, and on the tree hung an apple that shone in the sun as though it were pure gold. Then she went to the tree and plucked the apple as easily as though it were a gooseberry, and as soon as she had plucked it another as good grew in its place. Being hungry she ate it, and thought that she had never eaten anything as good, for it tasted like pancake with honey and milk.

By-and-by the oldest sister came out of the house and looked around, but when she saw the beautiful tree with the golden apple hanging from it you can guess how she stared.

Presently she began to long and long for the apple as she had never longed for anything in her life. "I will just pluck it," said she, "and no one will be the wiser for it." But that was easier said than done. She reached and reached, but she might as well have reached for the moon. She climbed and climbed, but she might as well have climbed for the sun—for either one would have been as easy to get as that which she wanted. At last she had to give up trying for it, and her temper was none the sweeter for that, you may be sure.

After a while came the second sister, and when she saw the golden apple she wanted it just as much as the first had done. But to want and to get are very different things, as she soon found, for she was no more able to get it than the other had been.

•••

Last of all came the mother, and she also strove to pluck the apple. But it was no use. She had no more luck of her trying than her daughters. All that the three could do was to stand under the tree and look at the apple, and wish for it and wish for it.

They are not the only ones who have done the like, with the apple of contentment hanging just above them.

As for Christine, she had nothing to do but to pluck an apple whenever she wanted it. Was she hungry? There was the apple hanging in the tree for her. Was she thirsty? There was the apple. Cold? There was the apple. So you see, she was the happiest girl betwixt all the seven hills that stand at the ends of the earth, for nobody in the world can have more than contentment, and that was what the apple brought her.

One day a king came riding along the road, and all of his people with him.

···

He looked up and saw the apple hanging
in the tree, and a great desire came upon
him to have a taste of it. So he called
one of the servants to him, and told him
to go and ask whether it could be bought
for a potful of gold.

So the servant went to the house, and
knocked on the door—rap! tap! tap!

"What do you want?" said the mother
of the three sisters, coming to the door.

Oh, nothing much, only a king was out
there in the road, and wanted to know if
she would sell the apple yonder for a
potful of gold.

Yes, the woman would do that. Just pay
her the pot of gold and he might go and
pluck it and welcome.

So the servant gave her the pot of gold,
and then he tried to pluck the apple. First
he reached for it, and then he climbed
for it, and then he shook the limb.

But it was no use for him to try. He
could no more get it—well—than *I* could
if I had been in his place.

···

At last the servant had to go back to the King. The apple was there, he said, and the woman had sold it, but try and try as he would he could no more get it than he could get the little stars in the sky.

Then the King told the steward to go and get it for him, but the steward, though he was a tall man and a strong man, could no more pluck the apple than the servant.

So he had to go back to the King with an empty fist. No, he could not gather it, either.

Then the King himself went. He knew that he could pluck it—of course he could! Well, he tried and tried, but nothing came of his trying, and he had to ride away at last without having had so much as a smell of the apple.

•••

After the King came home, he talked
and dreamed and thought of nothing but
the apple; for the more he could not get
it the more he wanted it—that is the way
we are made in this world. At last he grew
melancholy and sick for want of that
which he could not get. Then he sent for
one who was so wise that he had more in
his head than ten men together. This wise
man told him that the only one who could
pluck the fruit of contentment for him
was the one to whom the tree
belonged. This was
one of the daughters

of the woman who had sold the apple to him for the pot of gold.

When the King heard this he was very glad. He had his horse saddled, and he and his court rode away, and so came at last to the cottage where Christine lived. There they found the mother and the elder sisters, for Christine was away on the hills with her geese.

The King took off his hat and made a fine bow.

The wise man at home had told him this and that; now to which one of her daughters did the apple tree belong? so said the King.

"Oh, it is my oldest daughter who owns the tree," said the woman.

So, good! Then if the oldest daughter would pluck the apple for him he would take her home and marry her and make a queen of her. Only let her get it for him without delay.

Prut! that would never do. What! was the girl to climb the apple tree before

the King and all of the court? No! no!
Let the King go home, and she would
bring the apple to him all in good
time; that was what the woman said.

Well, the King would do that, only
let her make haste, for he wanted
it very much indeed.

As soon as the King had gone, the
woman and her daughters sent for
the goose-girl to the hills. Then they
told her that the King wanted the apple

yonder, and that she must pluck it for her sister to take to him. If she did not do as they said they would throw her into the well. So Christine had to pluck the fruit, and as soon as she had done so the oldest sister wrapped it up in a napkin and set off with it to the King's house, as pleased as pleased could be. Rap! tap! tap! she knocked at the door. Had she brought the apple for the King?

Oh yes, she had brought it. Here it was, all wrapped up in a fine napkin.

After that they did not let her stand outside the door till her toes were cold, I can tell you. As soon as she had come to the King she opened her napkin. Believe me or not as you please, all the same, I tell you that there was nothing in the napkin but a hard round stone. When the King saw only a stone he was so angry that he stamped like a rabbit and told them to put the girl out of the house. So they did, and she went home with a flea in her ear, I can tell you.

Why does the apple of contentment become a stone when the oldest daughter gives it to the King?

...

Then the King sent his steward to the house where Christine and her sisters lived.

He told the woman that he had come to find whether she had any other daughters.

Yes, the woman had another daughter, and, to tell the truth, it was she who owned the tree. Just let the steward go home again and the girl would fetch the apple in a little while.

As soon as the steward had gone, they sent to the hills for Christine again. Look! she must pluck the apple for the second sister to take to the King. If she did not do that they would throw her into the well.

So Christine had to pluck it, and gave it to the second sister, who wrapped it up in a napkin and set off for the King's house. But she fared no better than the other, for, when she opened the napkin, there was nothing in it but a lump of mud. So they packed her home again with her apron to her eyes.

∙∙∙

After a while the King's steward came to the house again. Had the woman no other daughter than these two?

Well, yes, there was one, but she was a poor ragged thing, of no account, and fit for nothing in the world but to tend the geese.

Where was she?

Oh, she was up on the hills now tending her flock.

But could the steward see her?

Yes, he might see her, but she was nothing but a poor simpleton.

That was all very good, but the steward would like to see her, for that was what the King had sent him there for.

So there was nothing to do but to send to the hills for Christine.

After a while she came, and the steward asked her if she could pluck the apple yonder for the King.

Yes, Christine could do that easily enough. So she reached and picked it

as though it had been nothing but a
gooseberry on the bush. Then the steward
took off his hat and made her a low
bow in spite of her ragged dress, for he
saw that she was the one for whom they
had been looking all this time.

So Christine slipped the golden apple
into her pocket, and then she and the
steward set off to the King's house
together.

When they had come there everybody
began to titter and laugh behind the

palms of their hands to see what a poor
ragged goose-girl the steward had brought
home with him. But for that the steward
cared not a rap.

"Have you brought the apple?" said
the King, as soon as Christine had come
before him.

Yes, here it was, and Christine thrust
her hand into her pocket and brought it
forth. Then the King took a great bite of it,
and as soon as he had done so he looked
at Christine and thought that he had never
seen such a pretty girl. As for her rags,
he minded them no more
than one minds the
spots on a cherry.

That was because he had eaten of the apple of contentment.

And were they married? Of course they were! And a grand wedding it was, I can tell you. It is a pity that you were not there, but though you were not, Christine's mother and sisters were, and, what is more, they danced with the others, though I believe they would rather have danced upon pins and needles.

"Never mind," said they. "We still have the apple of contentment at home, though we cannot taste of it." But no, they had nothing of the kind. The next morning it stood before the young Queen Christine's window, just as it had at her old home, for it belonged to her and to no one else in all of the world.

•••

That was lucky for the King, for he
needed a taste of it now and then as
much as anybody else, and no one
could pluck it for him but Christine.

Now, that is all of this story.
What does it mean? Can you not see?
Prut! rub your spectacles and
look again!

*Why does
the King still
need a taste
of the apple of
contentment
"now and
then"?*

ACKNOWLEDGMENTS

All possible care has been taken to trace ownership and secure permission for each selection in this series. The Great Books Foundation wishes to thank the following authors, publishers, and representatives for permission to reprint copyrighted material:

THE HAPPY LION, by Louise Fatio. Copyright 1954 by Louise Fatio Duvoisin and Roger Duvoisin; renewed 1982 by Louise Fatio Duvoisin. Reprinted by permission of the author.

Kanga and Baby Roo Come to the Forest, and Piglet Has a Bath, from WINNIE-THE-POOH, by A. A. Milne. Copyright 1926 by E. P. Dutton; renewed 1954 by A. A. Milne. Reprinted by permission of Dutton Children's Books, a division of Penguin Books USA, Inc.

Arap Sang and the Cranes, from TALES TOLD NEAR A CROCODILE, by Humphrey Harman. Copyright 1962 by Humphrey Harman. Reprinted by permission of Century Hutchinson Publishing Group Limited.

BLUE MOOSE, by Daniel Manus Pinkwater. Copyright 1975 by Daniel Manus Pinkwater. Reprinted by permission of G. P. Putnam's Sons.

Anancy and Dog and Puss and Friendship, from SPIDERMAN ANANCY, by James Berry. Copyright 1988 by James Berry. Reprinted by permission of Henry Holt and Company, Inc.

The Magic Listening Cap, from THE MAGIC LISTENING CAP: MORE FOLK TALES FROM JAPAN, by Yoshiko Uchida. Copyright 1955 by Yoshiko Uchida. Reprinted by permission of the author.

The Jackal and the Partridge, from TALES FROM THE PUNJAB, by Flora Annie Steel. Published by Macmillan Publishers (UK) Limited.

Nail Soup, by Linda Rahm. Copyright 1992 by The Great Books Foundation.

ILLUSTRATION CREDITS

Leo and Diane Dillon prepared the illustrations for *How the Camel Got His Hump*.

Frank Gargiulo prepared the illustrations for *Nail Soup*.

Patti Green prepared the illustrations for *The Jackal and the Partridge*.

David Johnson prepared the illustrations for *Jack and the Beanstalk*.

Barbara McClintock prepared the illustrations for *Anancy and Dog and Puss and Friendship*.

Daniel Manus Pinkwater's illustrations for *Blue Moose* are from the book of the same name. Reprinted by permission of G. P. Putnam's Sons.

Beatrix Potter's illustrations for *The Tale of Squirrel Nutkin* are from the book of the same name, first published in 1903 by Frederick Warne & Co.

Howard Pyle's illustrations for *The Apple of Contentment* are from PEPPER & SALT, OR SEASONING FOR YOUNG FOLK, by Howard Pyle, first published in 1885 by Harper & Brothers.

Ward Schumaker prepared the illustrations for *The Happy Lion*.

David Shannon prepared the illustrations for *Arap Sang and the Cranes*.

Ernest Shepard's illustrations for *Kanga and Roo Come to the Forest, and Piglet Has a Bath* are from WINNIE-THE-POOH. Reprinted by permission of Dutton Children's Books, a division of Penguin Books USA, Inc. Reproduced courtesy of the Newberry Library.

Ed Young prepared the illustrations for *The Magic Listening Cap*.